ACHIEVING SUCCESS

AGAINST

ALL

ODDS

ELOHOR EFFIONG (DR.)

"Winners never quit and quitters never win." - Vince Lombardi

For Michelle, my daughter and friend;

And for Makayla, my Sunshine through the rain.

TABLE OF CONTENTS

ACKNOWLEDGEMENT

Pastor David Ibiyeomie, my pastor and inspirer.

The MPH Class of 2014, Johns Hopkins Bloomberg School of Public Health, for keeping my vision alive.

And every author who has inspired me; especially, Prof. Ben Carson, my mentor.

Finally, every one going through tough times, keep the faith; I assure you, there is sunshine after the rain.

PREFACE

Facing challenges and winning is one of the toughest things we have to do in life. Everyone encounters difficulty, even in accomplishing the simplest of tasks. However, for some, the very essence of life is threatened by the seeming potent fear of failure. One of the most painful experiences a man can have is the feeling that he has failed. We can overcome the labels that others may place on us; we may be able to deal with knowing that our loved ones consider us failures but the despair that follows our acceptance that we have amounted to nothing is untamable.

"The spirit of a man will sustain his infirmity; but a wounded spirit who can bear?" (Proverbs 18:14)

Success is not a destination. Regardless of the troubles we face, or the difficulties that line our journeys to excellence, the truth remains absolute. There's no man who firmly believed in his heart that he would succeed that ended up a failure. Our circumstances are diverse but our survival mechanism is the same. Beating the odds to succeed is not abstract.

I attest to the possibility of success despite challenges and this is the very premise on which this book is built.

I sincerely believe that the principles contained within are universal. They are conscious practices that can be applied to any situation to achieve results. As I completed the framework for this book and proceeded to study the lives of the men before me, I found that although adaptation mechanisms may become refined over time, the necessities for survival are the same and inherent in all men.

Anyone can apply the stated principles to reach success.

Never let circumstance define you. Stand your ground, knowing that *"impossible is nothing."*

CHAPTER ONE
THE POWER OF OUR WORDS & THOUGHTS

I have read tons of stories about the positive outcome of our words. I have read the biographies of men who literally spoke their wealth and prosperity into being. Others have overcome debilitating illnesses by simply confessing health instead of disease. I call this the psychological warfare for success. The world's wealthiest men are simply those who refused to bow out in the face of certain failure. Some have faced bankruptcy but refused to give up. They envisioned their future, held their dream in their hearts, and spoke it till the universe yielded to them. In Christianity, we call it "the word of faith;" in the secular world, it is called "positive thinking." Either way, it works; ask Kenneth Copeland or Norman Vincent Peale. In actual fact, the word of faith begins with positive thinking. Declaring your positive thought gives it life to become the word of faith. If you don't think it, you can't confess it.

Our words are like bonds. They express our innermost thoughts and channel the course of our lives. That is why many authors and charismatic speakers have tried to get people to restructure their thought process and only speak out positivity. I know that positive speaking is effective. I attest to it.

"Death and life are in the power of the tongue." (Proverbs 18:21)

Here's the bad news: there is power in negativity too! As much as positive outcomes follow positive confessions, so do negative outcomes, with negative thoughts or confessions.

"How do I know this?"

Six years ago, I began researching the best schools of public health in the world. I had just completed medical school and was going through my internship in the College hospital where I had trained to become a doctor. During this period, I decided that I would rather be out in the field; taking health care to those in need than continue in the earlier path I had chosen to become a cosmetic Surgeon. In the course of my search, I found the Johns Hopkins University School of Public Health to have been the best school of Public health for two decades. I decided then, Hopkins it is; this was where I was going to study for a Master's degree in Public Health. This was where I would officially begin my public health career.

A year later, while serving as a Youths Corp officer in Northern Nigeria, precisely Maiduguri, I relayed my desire to my friends. I vividly remember someone asking how I was going to pay the tuition; my response was, "I want to see how I'll get admitted to Hopkins and God won't provide the fees." It probably doesn't sound like a good plan to anyone. But that was my best plan. My mind wandered on several options for covering the bill but nothing was set in stone.

Two years after my Youth's Corp service, I was admitted to the Johns Hopkins Bloomberg School of Public Health. Several months before I got accepted in Hopkins, I had begun preparations to go to Boston University, where I had been accepted with a partial scholarship. I eventually turned down Boston because the Bloomberg School of Public Health was my dream school. Going to Hopkins was neither a mistake nor chance occurrence. It was an event I spoke into being. I had said it repeatedly that I would receive my MPH degree at Hopkins. Before I got my acceptance letter from Hopkins, the University of London, an equally prestigious school, had also accepted my application and granted me admission. But Hopkins remained on my lips, and as I continued to say it, it happened. When the acceptance letter came in, I dropped every other offer and moved. There wasn't any other choice, for me. The one year I spent at the Bloomberg school of Public Health turned out to be the toughest in my life but it is an experience that will stay with me. More importantly however, I had exercised one of the powers given to man, calling forth a thing into existence.

I have had many of such experiences in my life and I know for sure that I am not alone. Many of us have called something to be, in times past, be it good or bad; or whether we were even aware of it or not. How many times have you mentioned wanting a thing and then inexplicably seen it happen? It could have been through prayer, purposeful speech or even careless conversation; but it came to pass anyway

I once had a truly funny experience. On the way to drop my older daughter off at school one morning, I noticed my toddler, being very playful and happy. It was only past 6am in the morning, and I expected her to be sleepy. Instead, she was moving around happily and playfully on the backseat of the car, almost too happily. So I uttered the words, *"why are you **too** happy this morning?"* It happened like lightning. Her mood changed and she began to sulk. She made faces, pouted and was set to cry. I didn't scold her but my negative comment had taken effect. I had referred to her as *"too"* happy and so there was a reset. Fortunately, one of the persons in the car observed what had happened and pointed out the effect of my words. Immediately, I took back my words and said, *"Please be happy again."* The switch was just as swift. She went back to being playful very quickly.

In 1997, David Ibiyeomie, the Pastor and founder of Salvation Ministries Worldwide, moved from Lagos to Port Harcourt, Nigeria, to begin his ministry. On his arrival, he paid out his entire savings as rent deposit and was left with no money in the bank or his pocket. The couple of years that followed saw him battle extreme poverty to the point of being unable to put food on the table. But he refused to give up and everyday he called himself a millionaire. Back then, he barely had good clothes on his back yet he would continuously say *"I am rich; I am very rich."* Today, he's one of the wealthiest and highest giving ministers in the world.

There is power in our tongue.

Word Power

About eleven years ago, Lucy (not real name) a good friend and classmate of mine got pregnant out of wedlock. She went through a very tough time dealing with external acceptance because the African society severely frowns at single motherhood and considers it scandalous. The African family values are deeply entrenched in a religious culture with the norm being, "wedding before babies." Any event outside of this normative expectation is hardly condoned and the ostracization that follows is often intense. Unwedded mothers are considered morally loose and treated as such. It is something akin to being an outcast or object of ridicule. It was even worse for Lucy because she is a Christian and was a Church leader. Her parents were of high standing in the Church and her family was well known. Many felt she had let them down and disgraced the faith. The immense and forgiving grace of God practiced by men, is seldom extended to women in such situations. Like others before her, Lucy was castigated and became a caricature for exemplification to other females.

In the midst of her turmoil, I called Lucy aside to have a tête-à-tête. She had handled the scandal quite well and I had a lot of respect for her. In the midst of our conversation, I simply said the words *"I want to have a baby."* I was in a stable relationship then and though I believed "he was the one," marriage wasn't on the radar. I just wanted a cute little baby to love. From that moment, that fate was sealed for me. It didn't make any difference that Lucy begged me not to. Her pleas didn't even matter to me. I had said I wanted a baby. I spoke out my desires and the universe heard me. It was up to "time and chance" to dictate when and where it would happen. It took some years, but I eventually got what I said; my baby, out of wedlock.

The spoken word requires a second component for manifestation. It comes into effect when it is accompanied by a heartfelt desire. A negative confession however, does not require the mind or heart for effect. I do not like to elaborate on the forces of evil, working extra hard to ensure "that time and chance happen," but suffice it to say that the odds are seemingly stacked in favor of failure and the slightest acknowledgement bespeaks the acceptance of negativity. It seems so much easier to fail than to succeed. You don't even need to think it, just say it. On the other hand, positivity requires more effort; so that success has to be worked for, yearned for and consistently reached for. It requires a conscious effort to say it right. It's just the way it is. Success begins from the mind and is then spoken forth.
You may wonder why positivity also requires the mind.

"... What things soever ye desire, when ye pray, believe that 7
First you desire (use your mind/heart) and then you pray (speak the word/ask). Just saying/asking is not enough; your mind needs to be engaged as well.

Was there a lesson to be learnt from my experience? Is there something I could have said and desired differently? Certainly. Did I learn my lesson? Definitely.

Two days before I finally decided to write this book, my daughter walked up to me and asked, *"Mommy, did you get married before you had me?"* The horns zonked in my head but I calmly answered *"No."* She is only seven and beginning to dig deep to the root of matters. My duty is to teach her and guide her right.

I do not regret being a single mother at that time; I chose to be one but I have learnt to use my tongue correctly. Part of my life's work is dedicated to helping single mothers. I have a genuine burden and admiration for any mother who is raising a child/children alone. It is one of the toughest things to do. I was a single mom by choice but that didn't make my life easier. I had a lot of help from my partner and eventually, family, but it didn't stop society from marring or labeling me. Truth is, parenthood was never intended for one person. That is why it takes two to make one; but circumstance may sometimes define our paths.

For every single mom raising her kid right, through emotional and social trauma, I raise my hand to you. I know your pain; I felt it too. You're two times a parent and that makes you almost superhuman. Hardly anyone knows how tough your days go or how hard you hit your pillows at night. Let your consolation be, that just like Ben Carson and Barack Obama, your child too can become a legend. Do it right. Speak and desire positivity in your children's lives. That daddy is not home, is no excuse for failure.

I found out I was pregnant with child on my mom's birthday. I had mixed feelings, unsure what the future held for me. I had to put the test-kit aside and embark on the three-hour journey to go celebrate my mom with family and friends.

A couple of weeks after my mom's birthday, the picture of my predicament became clearer. I was going to be a mom and I wasn't ready to get married. I was in my 5th year of Medical school and the last thing I needed was for anyone in my family to throw a tantrum that would negatively impact my performance at school or send me into depression for that matter. And that was highly probable.

Becoming a doctor was important to me and I wasn't ready to let go of the tight routine that had worked so well for me. I was involved in a relationship but that was about the beginning and end of my social life. I felt I could control a baby; I thought being a mom would be easy but to be both mom and wife was scary. Believe it or not, I was scared to get married. Forever was a long time to commit to. It was just the way my mind worked; the way my spoken words brought everything else into effect. I chose to forego a wedding.

It was my decision at that time and I believe it worked for me. I wasn't a wife, so I didn't need to perform any wifely duties. I didn't need to make meals for anyone, do house chores or whatever else wives did. I shut down on everything else so that all I had to do was care for myself and focus on school. I thought that would be pretty easy. I was wrong! I had one of the most difficult pregnancies I've ever witnessed, both as a person and doctor.

It is interesting to narrate now, but back then, it was a battle. For starters, I had a severe case of *hyperemesis gravidarum.* It was so bad I initially thought I had conceived twins but it turned out to be singleton. I had countless episodes of hematemesis (blood in vomitus) and food phobia. I can't remember how many doses of *Promethazine (Phenergan)* I received. I was constantly on intravenous fluid infusion during my first trimester and so it was common for *promethazine* to be injected in the infusions. That continued until I realized I suffered episodes of *akathisia,* a well-documented but very inconvenient side effect of intravenous promethazine, after each infusion.

While I pondered my decision to have a baby, I knew it was the best thing to do. I didn't want to have an induced abortion. In many countries all over the world, induced abortion is a crime. The procedure is also fraught with complications but these weren't my fears. Many people undergo the procedure hourly and move on with their lives. But somehow, my thought trend refused to follow the logical and socially correct path.

My confession had just come to pass. My words and thoughts were so powerful that they had produced another being!

While preparing the manuscript for this book, I did some research and was shocked by a Bible verse that most of us conveniently overlook. I intend to make a post card out of it, and stick it on the bathroom mirror as a daily reminder.

"But I say unto you, that every idle word that men shall speak, they shall give account thereof in the Day of Judgment. For by thy words thou shalt be justified, and by thy words thou shalt be condemned." (Matthew 12:36-37)

If you need more proof of word power, just remember that God spoke our existence, the entire world and all in it, into being. We were created in His image and we carry this essence, whether we are aware of it or not. We need to learn to master our tongues. Basically, every desire I have repeatedly uttered since my childhood has come to pass in my life. Most women get so exasperated with their situations that they utter careless words, against their children or partners and are then dismayed when these utterances begin to manifest. Speak only that which you desire to see fulfilled. We are mini-creators, not equal with God but certainly carrying His essence. Use it wisely.

The Fear of Failure

"For the thing which I greatly feared is come upon me, and that which I was afraid of is come unto me." (Job 3:25)

Fear is an overpowering influence on the mind. It is a negative emotion spurred by perceived threat. Once negativity sets in, it initiates a cascade of psychological reactions that prompt fearful actions. As a result, different emotions, including sadness, anxiety or panic may prevail. Very often, the victim turns his back and runs away from achieving his purpose because of the sense of danger relayed by the fear emotion on his mind. The fear of failure, also known as atychiphobia, causes its victims to live an enclosed, restricted life, unwilling to take risks even when they may be able to succeed. The fear is so intense that they quit trying to achieve, bury their potential and fail to live a meaningful life. Fear and the fear of failure are two elements in a related cascade. Fear may serve as a physiological mechanism that allows its victim to sense danger and move him to safety. However, to achieve success in life, fear must be completely controlled.

Fear and faith are two opposite sides of a coin. Heads (faith) you win, tails (fear) you lose. It's your pick. Both are powerful weapons, achieving that which stimulates them. Faith is built from hope and geared towards achieving whilst fear is built from insecurities and tends towards failure. Faith is hope put into action. Faith is borne when a man moves from the point of expectancy to acting like he has received. A man acts out faith when he moves back his living room chairs and creates a formation leaving space in the middle because he knows in his heart that the coffee table he desires will soon show up. He moves from wishful thinking to acting like he has received delivery of his table. He advertently gets it.

On the other hand, he may tend from wanting a table to fretting because his pay in the upcoming months is fully budgeted. He has outstanding bills to settle and sees no way of owning the table. Instead of keeping a positive outlook, he fills his mind with doubts. He gets no table. It is that simple; and it happens to the best of us.

I was served quite a number of eviction notices during my year at Hopkins. The first time I received an eviction notice, I refused to accept that I would move out of the apartment. I had no money and there was virtually no way in sight to make the payment. The apartment was a bit pricey and though certain circumstances had influenced our decision to rent it, I wasn't ready to begin house hunting or have "evicted" put next to my name on any record. The thought of loosing one's home under any circumstance can be demoralizing. It is one thing to not have food on the table but to have your roof taken away from over your head is something else. I hoped against hope. I fought the deepening fear in my heart and spoke my desire for days on end. On the court date, I received money from home to pay for two months rent. When my husband called me that morning to say he was going to send me money, I was a bit skeptical but when he mentioned the amount, I knew that faith had paid off.

The subsequent month, I received another notice and I handled it with the same principle. I was downcast about the lack we experienced but refused to let my mind think we would be homeless. The court date came but I didn't have the money. The day before we were scheduled for eviction, I said to my six-year old daughter on the way back from her school, *"let's hurry home and pack our stuff."*
She looked at me and asked me, *"Mom do you want to leave?"* I answered in the negative. And the she said, *"then stop saying it; expect your miracle."* Wow! *Out of the mouths of babes and sucklings..."* (Psalm 8:2)

Her words strengthened me and even though it was only a few hours before the Sherriff was scheduled to kick us out, we didn't pack. To make matters worse, my mom had to come to visit and I did not want her to experience the drama that could ensue. I intimated her of the situation but asked her not to pack a thing. On the morning of the proposed eviction, I dropped my daughter off at school and went back to my apartment. The eviction was scheduled for 9am. Thirty minutes before the time, my miracle came through. Once again, faith prevailed.

However, when I was served another notice for the third time in a row, I gave up. I allowed fear and frustration to set in and take control of my mind. My husband's business hadn't picked up and I was yet to receive my work permit. Despite the previous miracles, I could not believe that help would come. I shut my heart to a miracle from God, restricting my options without being fully aware of my actions. I mentally packed my stuff and began to search for transitional housing. On the morning of the eviction, I moved my kids and I into a homeless shelter. There is hardly a clearer demonstration of the power of fear and faith than what I experienced. The results were the simplest manifestation of what I allowed to fill my mind. It is the same with other situations in which we find ourselves. Fear disrupts or delays our successes and this remains until we let hope come alive.

My experience within the housing we moved into was both amusing and degrading. I eventually discovered it was a house meant for recovering addicts. In other words, it was a semi-rehabilitation center. I had no idea of the fact before I moved in and the house manager cleverly hid it from me.

Amidst battling this revelation, one of the house officers, a girl, barely out of her teens treated everyone like scum. We were not allowed to sit on the chairs or own more than one loaf of bread at anytime.

Even though the house manager assured me she had cleaners who worked round the clock before she took whatever money I had on me, her officer asked me to scrub out the bathroom floor or pick a different chore. My mind was worse than a whirlpool. I refused to enter my name as a resident and knew I had to get my kids out of there. But how? I was left with less money than I had when I moved into the house. Within 48hours of being in the house, I realized myself. On the morning of the third day, I said to my daughter, *"We are leaving this house today."* She responded with an *"Amen."*

I still had no idea how. As a matter of fact, I had no more money on me except for the $20 left in my purse. But I said it and meant it. I used two powerful unfailing weapons, the word of mouth/positive thinking and faith. I went through the day unconscious of my declaration that morning but my innermost desire had been in line with my confession and faith. The thing that I feared the most had happened to me so fear no longer had a stronghold over me. There were no what "ifs" or what if not. *He that is down needs fear no fall.* I could have chosen to doubt my declaration but I didn't even have the time to consider it. I got my kids and myself ready and went downtown, just to be out of the building.

The events that occurred later that evening were less than amusing but suffice it to say that I did not spend another night in that shelter. Just before midnight, my bags were moved out of the house and I got checked into a hotel. I had gotten another miracle as God sent His servant to our rescue. It took a while before what had happened made any sense in my head. When I finally remembered, I turned to my daughter and asked, *"Do you remember what we said yesterday morning?"* She said *"yes."*

Recall the story of how Peter walked on water (Matthew 14:28-30) and you'll understand the role of fear in our lives, careers, relationships, and business. I don't know about you but I want to walk on water and not sink. As a teenager, my friends and I coined some sayings from simple words. We would say things like, *"The difference between the ordinary and extraordinary is the extra before the ordinary."*

I have never been satisfied with the ordinary. I broke out from a family of persons who wrote their school leaving certificate exams more than once to become the first to accomplish it in the first try. I came out from among the midst of people who struggled to get a first degree to become the first to graduate with a summa cum laude equivalent. In the midst of seemingly enlightened individuals I became the first to progress to receive a doctoral degree. In spite of the obstacles I faced, I successfully completed my postgraduate education in a world-class school, the best in its field. At every point, the hurdles in my path seemed insurmountable. My way was marked with fearfulness, which was deeply aroused by the threats before me. In this book, I pour out my experiences and share all the weapons and principles that helped me succeed.

Fear is conquerable. No matter the insubstantiality of your background, if you set your heart to fly, fly you will. Never allow fear overpower your mind. It is only as powerful as you allow. Positive thinking and declaration (word of faith) may not always suffice in conquering fear. But a combination of these with the word of God never fails. Every time I desired something and fear seemed to envelope me, I started the warfare with my thoughts (positive thinking), and then I declared it (word of faith), and as fear threatened my faith, I built it even more with the word of God and prayer. These strengthened my resolve to battle any odds and reach for what I desired. The weapons never failed. Fear is only an emotion. You're the commander who can bring it to life or rip it to shreds. The choice is yours.

Power in the Word

By this, I refer to the power in the word of God, specifically in the spoken Word. Recently, I had the opportunity of praying with some persons over the phone and I constantly reminded them of the power that God's word holds over every situation that we are faced with. It's not my intention to preach but I'll be the most selfish and dishonest person if I refuse to share the role that God's word has played in my life.

All of my successes have been rooted in a walk with God, perfect or imperfect. I have been blessed with persons who hold me up with a constant supply of God's word when any ground beneath me is about to crumble and the one person who has played this role best is my husband.

When I was admitted into the Johns Hopkins University (JHU) to study for my MPH degree, I received a scholarship from an independent organization for thirty thousand USD. It was a lot of money. But my projected expenditure for the year was about eighty-nine thousand USD. I needed an extra fifty-nine thousand USD to float this dream. At the time, my husband's construction business was in good shape and he had several partnerships that were guaranteed to bring in millions of dollars. We considered the situation and decided we could handle it. I had also been nominated for an honorary award to be given by the President of Nigeria, for having being the best Corp's member when I served under the National Youth Service Corps in Borno State in 2010. The award had a scholarship benefit attached to it, so I felt somewhat comfortable.

In as short as a few months, my world crumbled. My husband's business suffered a huge set back that caused him and several other investors to lose a lot of money. To make matters worse, I failed to receive the award and never got the scholarship. My dream began to fade in front of me.

A couple of months before the beginning of the school year at Hopkins, I decided to write the admissions office to get a deferment but my husband wouldn't hear of it. He told me in simple terms, *"you will not do that; you will go to school."*

I am not sure what gave him confidence but I chose to believe him. Two months later, he received a check worth ninety thousand USD as payment for a job he had done. The check was received two days before my flight out of Nigeria to the U.S.A. Our plan was simple. He would wire money to me as soon as the check cleared. That way, I was sure to get some money as soon as I arrived the U.S. The timing was brilliant but there was a snag; the check never paid out!

I arrived the U.S, heavily pregnant, and in the company of my five-year old daughter with only enough money to last a couple of weeks. We were stranded! There wasn't even money for return tickets! Besides, returning home without accomplishing what I came for wasn't part of the plan. Thankfully, I had $30,000 in scholarship funds and so I didn't have to immediately worry about tuition. I'll save the story of our survival for subsequent chapters but first let me share how God's word brought my dream at Hopkins to fruition.

February 21st 2014 is etched on my mind forever. For as long as I have breath in my lungs, the day I saw God move extraordinarily to bring about a miracle using strangers will never be forgotten.

I began lectures at the JHU in July 2013 and by the end of September, my scholarship had run out. We had lived by faith and hoped against hope that my husband's business situation would turn around; that debtors would pay up or that other monies would be remitted to ease our need but nothing happened. Taking the return flight home or quitting midway wasn't an option, so I forged on. In October of 2013, my student's account got blocked for the first time due to insufficient funds. I could not register for the upcoming term and this posed dire consequences for my non-immigrant status. Fortunately, a call to the student's account manager bought me a few more weeks and permission to register. But by January 2014 my luck ran out.

I had taken the initiative to inform the school authorities of my situation. I tried to explain that I had not come into the U.S.A on false pretexts but that fate had dealt a distressing hand in my current situation. I tried to ask for more time while frantically searching out scholarships and other means to pay up my tuition. It was a waste of time. No one was interested or sympathized with my situation. At the end of January, I got the news from the office of international services, to either be registered at 5pm (Eastern time) on February 21st 2014 or have my immigration documents cancelled. This would force me into illegal non-immigrant status within the country. I'm not very smart at breaking laws. I had no other choice but to get registered.

Despite the inability to access my student account, I picked out my courses for the term and informed the faculty and teaching assistants for each course, of my situation and intention to officially complete registration before the term ran out. Luckily, l was allowed to sit in on lectures, take tests and submit assignments. I couldn't access courses online so the assistants had to mail me copies of lecture notes, assignments or tests. Eventually, the teaching assistants granted me special permission to access quiz sites online, as a guest. All my assignments had to be submitted via the faculty or teaching assistant's email instead of through the course sites. On some occasions, I sent copies to both to avoid conflict. It wasn't a pretty situation but not much had been since my arrival in the country. I now had two terms before graduation and wasn't about to give up. A few weeks into this routine, someone in the program office gave my friend a message for me; I was asked to stop attending classes. The message bothered me but the next day, I was in class. I didn't want to be found wanting when God's word came true. Besides, my miracle was for school; how would it meet me in the house? As difficult as it was, I determined to play my part.

The days passed quickly and February 21st stared me in the face. By February 20th, I had less than 24hours to cough up $11,000 or pack my bags. Pack my bags wasn't a workable choice. My baby, Kay, neither had her passport nor a Nigerian visa. I hadn't even picked up her birth certificate because every dollar I had gotten since I arrived was budgeted for and her birth certificate just couldn't top food on the scale of preference.

To cut the story short, at 12noon on February 21st 2014, I only had about $3,000 in the bank. The account office wasn't playing. I beat down the $11,000 to $10,000 but I didn't have that much either. While I travailed and broke within my spirit, my husband refused to believe or accept the situation. I tried so hard to make him understand the bleakness of it all but he just wouldn't. Instead he sent me a collection of Bible verses to empower my mind. I really didn't know how the verses were going to touch the students affair's Dean who had told me he doesn't go to Church; nor was I sure how the verses would raise the money I needed. All I wanted to see at that time were dollar signs. I completely forgot that, *"the*

Earth is the Lord's and the fullness thereof... (Psalm 24:1); *and the cattle upon a thousand hills."* (Psalm 50:10)

I got tons of messages intended to build my faith and reliance on God for the miracle I desperately needed. It was the toughest thing to do but my husband believed; I couldn't see the silver lining in the dark cloud but I decided to join my faith with his. We confessed the Word together. I had till 5pm February 21st to receive a miracle.

10:30am February 21st 2014

I had a meeting scheduled with the Dean of student affairs. My friend and classmate, a human's right professor and activist, Bee, had written the Dean of the School of Public Health on my behalf. Even though I was skeptical, she refused to back down. I was hoping to be allowed more time to pay up but Bee wanted a welfare scholarship. None of this happened. The message from the authorities that came through the student affairs Dean was simple, *"pay by 5pm today or leave."* Kay still didn't have her passport. I wasn't willing to be deported or become an illegal non-immigrant. I gave my husband the sour update; he gave me the Word. My hope was strong. I mentally calculated how I could raise the money, and hoped it worked out.

12:00 noon

Bee met with other classmates and they came up with the idea to raise funds though my class page on Facebook. They didn't want to see me go home. We had all come so far and May 20th was within sight.

I declined. I didn't want to risk getting in more trouble with the school authorities.

12:30pm

My classmates voted 3:1 against me, and overruled my decision to keep it out of Facebook and away from the class. According to them, *"you are going home anyway; you have nothing to lose."*

Right in front of me, a post went up on the class Facebook page. I walked away.

1:00pm

I got back to my apartment and got on the phone. I was frantic, I was desperate; I needed a swift miracle. I called up a few persons whom I believe could help. After an hour on the phone, I got nothing. I had $0 in addition to the $3,000 my mom had wired the previous day. It was now 2pm and I was none the better. I still needed $7,000. It was nowhere in sight!

2:00pm

I logged on to my class Facebook group page. There were minute-by-minute updates of how much had been raised and I hoped there was a miracle in there. My class had raised $300. I felt myself begin to shut down. I was beginning to switch mentation. The time was near. I was going to go home.

2:20pm

I took time out to cry while sitting in the lobby downstairs in my apartment complex. I thought of how to inform the authorities I didn't have the money and then pack my bags in preparation to leave. Kay still didn't have her passport or visa. I wasn't sure how to pay for return tickets. I decided I would walk into the Dean's office at 4pm and let him know I would be leaving. I tried to be strong. It wasn't working. I checked back on the class Facebook page, desperate and willing to see a miracle. There was none. There wasn't much progress made from the previous amount. I saw pleas from the few international students I was close to, calling on my classmates to *"please come on and do this."* I believe the aim was to get all 200 persons in my class to donate $35 each. It wasn't working. The time was too short. Not many people would have checked their Facebook in a space of two hours on a Friday. Definitely, not in a school like Hopkins, where the academic work, is often beyond tedious. I looked at the time again. The tears came pouring down like a dam had broken loose. I stood up, turned around to head upstairs to my apartment. And my phone rang.

2:30pm

I checked my Facebook account one more time to follow the progress. There was a message from someone who said he was racing down to give $300. It struck me, but it wasn't enough to save me. It wasn't enough to be my miracle.

Just then, I gave up completely. It was over. I knew my time at Hopkins had come to an end. Temporarily. In the midst of the tears and hopelessness, my mind whirred with plans. Suddenly, I heard my phone ring; it was Bee.

I took the call and got the shock of my life. Bee gave me her message in exactly these words, *"Elohor, we need you to come down to the School of Public Health; we have raised…, wait for it…, $6,000."*

The God of Abraham, Isaac and Jacob all over again… *"same God, yesterday, today and forever."* (Hebrews 13:8)

"I am the Lord God of all flesh, is anything too hard for me to do?" (Jeremiah 29:11)

"For I know the plans that I have concerning you, to give you a

hope and a future, to bring you to an expected end." (Jeremiah 32:27).

"Better is the end of a matter than the beginning..." (Ecclesiastes 7:8)

3:30pm

I got a call from the Dean of Student's affairs, asking me to show up because he was aware my classmates were raising the funds I needed. He wanted me in the student's affairs unit to fill out a paper form for the courses I needed to register, as I required special access because the deadline for registration was long overdue. I got my kids and headed for the bus stop. I didn't have the money to pay for a cab.

4:00pm

I was frantic to the point of passing out. The buses were late and I had to be done with registration by 5pm to beat the international office deadline. My classmates were blowing up my phone because they were worried sore. I was late and it wasn't a home run yet. If the office of international service could not access my account online by 5pm, that would be it. I got another reminder from the international office. They weren't playing; 5pm was it!

4:30pm

Whoosh! Relief! I exhaled as I got on the bus and headed to the School of Public Health.

I arrived barely in time and my colleagues had to go in the account office to deposit $10,000 on my behalf. Yeah, we made it up somehow.

I was promptly heralded by another group of classmates to the Dean's office. There was a hitch. The student affairs unit insisted they needed written permission from the faculty stating I had been attending classes and was permitted to register for the term. The request was genuine and reasonable. It was already 5weeks into the term and my registration was late. I needed to prove I had sat in on lectures for five weeks. But it was past 4pm on a Friday evening. Neither the faculty nor their teaching assistants were exactly sitting in their offices waiting to hand me permission slips. Even if they were, I couldn't round up on five offices and make it back to the registrar's office in 20minutes. Tick tock… time was running out.

4:55pm

I logged into the course site to reveal the special access I had been granted to take quizzes early on in the term. I wanted to register five courses for the term and the course site showed I had received special access and participated in all five classes. The access had been granted on the official school site. There was no reason to doubt or suspect foul play.

5:05pm

I was fully registered for the penultimate term to graduation. The Dean expressed his fears over my situation with the international office. I hadn't made the 5pm deadline. There was a chance my documents had been pulled. The moments leading up to my registration had been electrified with so much frenzy that I had neglected to inform the international office that I would be registered within the hour.

I saw a colleague motion to me from outside the office of student affairs. It was past work hours and so she wasn't allowed in. She wanted to know if I made it; if I was going to be part of the graduating class on May 20th. I didn't know. I had to contact the international office.

5:20pm

After several tries, I made it through to the international office via email. And I waited soberly for their response. What if I didn't make it? What if all the effort by my colleagues hadn't saved the day? What if I hadn't gotten a complete miracle?

"The blessing of the Lord, it maketh rich; and He addeth no sorrow." (Proverbs 10:22)

In less than 10 minutes, a call came through to the Dean's office from the International office. They needed to confirm my status. The Dean's staff gave an affirmative response to questions concerning my registration. That was it.

I made it. I was registered. I wasn't going to go home; I was still here. I was going to finish the term and my daughters and I were no longer threatened with possible deportation. It was a home run.

I fought; my husband and I prayed. I feared and tried to play God. But it was His Word that swung into action to create a miracle that the Chairman of the Public Health program was to later tell me *"has never happened in the history of our school."*

Apparently, everyone else who had been in my shoes was sent home (oh! Believe me, there were lots of people in my shoes!!)

5:40pm

I'm out of the office of student affairs and I meet up with colleagues who had dutifully sat with my kids while I was away. I got hugs from people I had never spoken to since my arrival at Hopkins.

There were tears in my eyes. Thank you would never be enough. My daughter who had prayed incessantly with me, crying for a miracle was overjoyed. She was glad mommy was now fine and that God showed up.

I learnt an important and powerful lesson, *"His Word is yea and Amen." (2 Corinthians 1:20)*

In the term that followed, I was faced with same scenario again. It was my final term and as usual I obtained permission to take classes till I could pay up my bills and be officially registered.

The MPH year had turned out to be the toughest and roughest in my entire life. After the events during the penultimate term to graduation, I was led to war against the situation using God's Word. I had seen His Word come alive and I was willing to trust Him fully this time. I sat down and wrote down my favorite promises from God's word. They were promises suited to my situation and verses that built my faith. I copied them all out on a sheet of paper and memorized them. Every time my heart shook in fear, Gods word arose within me, powered by the Holy Spirit. I would then turn my heart towards Him and keep the faith. But I must tell you this; it was light years away from easy. I cannot fully describe the sadness that often gripped me, nor the well of tears that never dried, I just know that I believed God is able and I had to keep pressing.

In the end, His word prevailed. The entire amount I needed to complete the term was paid and I fulfilled all academic requirements for graduation.

God's Word works wonders any day. In the words of my Pastor and spiritual father, Pastor David Ibiyeomie, *"I know it as I know my name."*

Below, I have included a list of my favorite scriptures for keeping faith. Feel free to make post cards and add your own faith inspiring scripture. Faith makes the word of God come alive; yes, His word truly comes live.

"Ah Lord God! behold, thou hast made the heaven and the earth by thy great power and stretched out arm, and there is nothing too hard for thee." (Jeremiah 32:17)

"Thou wilt keep him in perfect peace, whose mind is stayed on Thee, because he trusteth in Thee." (Isaiah 26:3)

"Better is the end of a thing than the beginning thereof:" (Ecclesiastes 7:8)

"Behold, the Lord's hand is not shortened, that it cannot save; neither His ear heavy, that it cannot hear." (Isaiah 59:1)

"To appoint unto them that mourn in Zion, to give unto them beauty for ashes, the oil of joy for mourning, the garment of praise for the spirit of heaviness, that they might be called trees of righteousness, the planting of the Lord, that He might be glorified." (Isaiah 61:3)

"I have set the Lord always before me; because He is at my right hand, I shall not be moved." (Psalm16:8)

"Who is he that saith, and it cometh to pass, when the Lord commandeth it not?" (Lamentations 3:37)

"He that spared not his own Son, but delivered him up for us all, how shall he not with him also freely give us all things?" (Romans 8:32)

"For I know the thoughts that I think toward you, saith the Lord, thoughts of peace and not of evil, to give you an expected end." (Jeremiah 29:11)

"No weapon that is formed against thee shall prosper; and every tongue that shall rise against thee in judgment thou shalt condemn. This is the heritage of the servants of the Lord, and their righteousness is of Me," saith the Lord." (Isaiah 54:11)

"I am the Lord, and there is none else; there is no God besides Me. I girded thee, though thou hast not known Me," (Isaiah 45:5)

"Behold, I am the Lord, the God of all flesh. Is there any thing too hard for Me?" (Jeremiah 32:27)
"For surely there is an end; and thine expectation shall not be cut off." (Proverbs 23:18)

"For verily I say unto you, that whosoever shall say unto this mountain, 'Be thou removed, and be thou cast into the sea,' and shall not doubt in his heart, but shall believe that those things which he saith shall come to pass, he shall have whatsoever he saith." (Mark 11:23)

"And Moses said unto the people, "Fear ye not. Stand still, and see the salvation of the Lord, which He will show to you today;" (Exodus 14:13)

"Bring ye all the tithes into the storehouse, that there may be meat in Mine house, and put Me to the proof now herewith," saith the Lord of hosts, "if I will not open to you the windows of heaven and pour you out a blessing, that there shall not be room enough to receive it.
And I will rebuke the devourer for your sakes, and he shall not destroy the fruits of your ground, neither shall your vine cast her fruit before the time in the field," saith the Lord of hosts. And all nations shall call you blessed, for ye shall be a delightsome land," saith the Lord of hosts." (Malachi 3:10-12)

"When thou passest through the waters, I will be with thee; and through the rivers, they shall not overflow thee: when thou walkest through the fire, thou shalt not be burned;" (Isaiah 43:2)

"Fear thou not; for I am with thee: be not dismayed; for I am thy God: I will strengthen thee; yea, I will help thee; yea, I will uphold thee with the right hand of my righteousness. For I the

Lord thy God will hold thy right hand, saying unto thee, Fear not; I will help thee."(Isaiah 41:10,13)

"So shall My word be that goeth forth out of My mouth: It shall not return unto Me void, but it shall accomplish that which I please, and it shall prosper in the thing whereto I sent it." (Isaiah 55:11)

And all things whatsoever ye shall ask in prayer, believing, ye shall receive." (Matthew 21:22)

Illustration Format: Positive thinking, word of faith and the power in God's word

iFormat 1

Arsenio wants a new car. He doesn't just want it; he actually needs it. He runs a private transport business for select clients but his present car is old and always at the mechanic. He needs a new luxury car to help with his business but his current finances cannot handle the purchase. He is the breadwinner in the family and thus has to ensure that his business continues to run in order to bring in the money to care for his family. He cannot take out a loan because previous financial need resulted in a personal bad credit history.

Application

There are many persons in similar situations. It may not be a car or any material thing. It may be a struggle to overcome disease, debt, or start up a new business/company. It may even be the need to continue in a current project. Whatever the case, there are solutions. Pull up a pen and paper, and use the iFormat as a template to develop your own powered positive mentality. It is a good start and it works.

1. Think of your desires, goals and needs

What is your mental attitude towards them? For instance, like Arsenio, you may need a new car, home or have other needs. How do you think about getting one? Do you think it is achievable or you think it impossible? Do you harbor any fears towards using or maintaining a new car? Why do you even need a new car?

2. Do you ever talk about owning a car? Do you say it positively or do you talk it down?

3. Do you truly desire owning this car? Does the thought of owning the car give you pleasure? Or are you nonchalant? Do you see another way out (back up plan)?

4. Have you found any promise in God's word to help strengthen your faith that you will get what you desire? Do you believe that God's plan and will allow you to achieve your dream?

5. How do you prepare for the arrival of your car?

Sample iFormat: illustrative answers to the iFormat1

1. Desire: I want a car

Need: I need a car

Goal: I am going to get the car in 3months/6months/1year

I know I can get this car. I can buy it and maintain it. I can handle the insurance and every other responsibility that comes with the car. It is going to be a big asset to my business and family.

2. Every morning while brushing my hair in front of the mirror, I smile and say to myself, I am the owner of a brand new metallic gray Lexus RX 330. I look in the mirror, and I see myself in my car. I say it every chance I get. I am going to gain more high profile clients and bring more money home to my family.

3. Today, I thought about my Lexus vehicle and my heart leaped. I look forward to driving it home. I see my car with mind's eye all the time. It's the first thing I see when I wake and the last thing on my mind when I go to bed. I'm going to accomplish it because I know I can. My Plan A is to get the car; plan B is to get the car; plan C is getting the car.

4. Today, I wondered if owning a Lexus car was out of place and if I could make do with something smaller. My business would surely receive better returns if I use such a car though. Wow! I just saw in God's word that I can have any thing I want (Jeremiah 29:7; 3John 1:2; John 14:14). Now, every time I talk about my car, I speak God's word too. I just know it's going to be a big asset to my business and family.

5. I just asked my wife and kids to join me in clearing out the garage. We will need the space for our new car.

Once you have the right thoughts, confessions and desire in place, the next thing is to resolve to work towards achieving your dream. The power of resolution is described in Chapter two.

CHAPTER TWO
DETERMINATION

The Merriam-Webster online dictionary defines determination as *"a quality that makes you continue trying to do or achieve something that is difficult."* Google defines it as *"firmness of purpose, resoluteness; the process of establishing something exactly, typically by calculation or research."* I define it as the ability to stay focused and not back down in the face of struggle.

Much as I like the definitions, I like the synonyms best. The synonyms have an appeal and appear so familiar. I look at words like willpower, backbone, intentness and single-mindedness and I feel like I'm looking at my name. For a long time now, my self-description on Facebook has been "I've got a diamond back; you can't break it!" Do I really have a diamond back? Can it be broken?

I do not think that any one person was born with determination. Although some people firmly believe that one has to be born with a particular amount of will power to grow determination, I politely disagree. I concur more with schools of thought who believe determination is a skill that can be learned. Determination is one of those traits the human race cultivates to survive and excel. If one must achieve a useful and challenging goal, then you must be ready to demonstrate a good measure of strength of character. There are several types of determination but I'll discuss the three main ones that are commonly exhibited.

Types of Determination

Uphill Determination: this is the type of determination demonstrated by someone who works to achieve a difficult task despite intense difficulties or obstacles. An example of this was when I worked to complete my term courses at Hopkins despite a broken leg, contralateral sprained ankle and the constant threats of cancellation of immigration documents by the office of international services. This kind of determination requires intense will power; it is exhausting and difficult to sustain over long periods of time. It is usually stimulated by a disposition to win at all costs but is not advised as the only practiced form of determination.

Downhill determination: this type of determination does not require a definite form of resolution but usually follows the path of least resistance. This type of determination accomplishes goals that are rarely the ones yearned for. A person who practices downhill determination has a desire to succeed but is open to various angles for doing so. As a result, he tends toward the path of least resistance or less challenge. While success is reached, the results are often not that which is wished for.

Coastal determination: Coastal determination requires self-discipline and is often the preferred form of determination because it is less exhausting than the uphill type. Coastal determination involves proactive measures that delay gratification in expectation of the realization of a desired goal. As a medical student, I would often read over my notes and texts on a daily basis in preparation for the final exams at the end of the year. This required a significant measure of self-discipline that necessitated the non-existence of a healthy social life, absence from family trips or reunions and fewer hours for much-desired sleep. My goal was defined as success during my final exams and I was determined to work towards it and achieve it. As such, I had to make the sacrifice to study daily.

A businessman practices this type of determination when he refrains from spending his profit and instead re-invests it in his business. The momentary pleasure he could have had in spending his profit on flashy cars, designer clothes or vacation becomes an ultimate sacrifice for the growth or expansion of his business.

Every one of us can relate to one or more types of determination that we may have practiced or currently practice. I have had to use uphill determination to overcome most of my recent challenges but usually I'm more pro coastal determination. I have never liked the easy way out of any situation and as such tend to gravitate away from practicing downhill determination. It is advantageous to practice a mix of different determination types, especially the coastal and uphill types, depending on what is required for a successful outcome.

Because determination can be learned and consciously applied, it is best to begin with defining what success means to you and setting timeline goals based on your expectations. Success means different thing to us. What constitutes success for one person may be abhorrent to another. Humans tackle challenges differently; therefore another's accomplishments should never be a yardstick for measuring your success. Our desires are completely different. When I began having serious issues during my MPH, an acquaintance told me, *"go home, living in America is not a do or die affair."* To dissect this, she had an end limit definition of success as "living comfortably in America or anywhere else in he world" but I had defined success as "achieving my MPH degree." Our expectations and approach were thus different.

The first task for today, this very moment, is to identify your goals. Pick up a pen and paper, and itemize one or more end goals, which will amount to success for you when achieved. It may be completing fashion school or an academic degree; it may also be building a house, getting employed or raising a family.

Task two: Put a timeline to achieving these goals.
Now think of two smaller goals under each major goal listed above and write them down. These small goals may or may not lie in the pathway of your major goals. The reason for the smaller goals is to maintain a sense of accomplishment that keeps you going. Otherwise, solely striving to achieve major success may drain or burn you out. From time to time, go back to that paper and read up what you have written. This is a good way to shape the future.

While my eyes were fixed on completing the requirements for my MPH, I had several other small goals that kept me in the game. I had to pass several courses each term; I had to ensure my kids were well cared for. I also started a health blog, which gave me a measure of pride and sense of fulfillment. These smaller, easy to accomplish goals kept me refreshed.

Typically, every goal should be embedded within a bigger goal. Why do you want to become a successful entrepreneur? Do you hope to become successful in your business in order to accomplish something else? It's almost easy for me to keep pressing in the paths that I have chosen and to use coastal or uphill determination skills to my advantage because I have an end goal that must be reached. Obtaining a Master's in Public Health was not my ultimate; it was a landmark that needed to be crossed while chasing my dream. I call the entire dream, the "big picture." If you desire to become a successful entrepreneur so you can be among the top businessmen in the world, you may get drained chasing the top; but if you include smaller achievable goals in the pathway, then some measure of success in your business will inspire you to keep going. Your eyes are on the "big picture" but you receive enough drive from your small successes to keep climbing.

Streamlining your focus: single-mindedness

Determination embodies several little traits. A determined person is a steadfast person, he is single minded and focused. He is unwavering; he presses on regardless of any hurdle in his way. Throw a spanner in the wheel, he will keep moving. Toss in a monkey wrench and he'll still make things happen. His eyes are on the prize and that is all he beholds. He has set his sights and he walks on the path towards them. He embraces challenges and overcomes them gainfully because success is his goal. On the other hand, a double minded man lacks focus. He rarely achieves anything meaningful because his actions bespeak spinelessness. He fixes his eyes on a venture but never sees it through to the end. He is desirous of one thing in a minute but is distracted by something else the next. He gets engaged to a beautiful hardworking woman but runs after everything in skirts. He has no virtue and is unset in all he does. The Bible clearly extols the virtue of single-mindedness, describing a double-minded man as *"unstable in his ways"* and incapable of receiving anything from God (James 1:7&8).

When I found I was pregnant in my fifth year of medical school, I remained unwavering in my expectations. Much like many first time pregnancies, mine was a difficult one. I had a goal; I was going to keep at school and have my baby. I wasn't ready to take any time off. It was no mean feat.

I asked God for three things daily, mostly for the baby I carried. These three requests were always on my lips every time I knelt down to pray. Oh, I knew I had no business talking to God. I was going to be a single mom; no wedding, no engagement, no ring. Nada! How dare I even mention I talked to God?

Well, I say this with a huge smile on my face, I did talk to Him, and apparently, even with all my sins, He heard me. That's the thing about God; He'll *"have mercy on whom He has mercy, and have compassion on whom He has compassion"* (Romans 9:15). Thankfully He answers to no one. If He did, mankind would be in a bigger mess than it is in today.

I went through my pregnancy without missing a single posting at school. Was it tough? Like hell it was. But I worked hard, I worked really hard, even with the difficulty I had with pregnancy symptoms and the absence of a solid support structure. A couple of weeks before my third professional exams, the Academic Staff Union of Universities (ASUU) went on strike. As a result, the academic blocks were shut down for one month. This was a wonderful window of opportunity to catch up on whatever lapses I had yet to cover in my academics. I went to the hospital seminar room everyday to read up everything I could on pediatrics and obstetrics and gynecology. When my colleagues took their rest or hung out in the clinical hostel, I had my swollen feet propped up on a chair in the obstetrics & gynecology seminar room with my lecture notes and medical texts for company. I attended all clinical tutorial classes offered by senior residents in the department of obstetrics and gynecology.

I was particularly disciplined going through every phase of college. I was often the student to whom struggling colleagues were referred. I didn't think highly of myself because I knew my inherent nature. My eyes were only focused on one prize: to achieve my MBBS. So I worked, and I prayed.

I was at a disadvantage, just by being an expectant mom during my pediatric rotations. While the obstetrics and gynecology unit didn't concern themselves much with their student's marital status, the pediatrics unit was notorious for doing just the opposite. You were considered to have misplaced priorities if married while in Medical school. A visible pregnancy during pediatric finals was definitely stretching your luck. The bad news was, the pediatrics department didn't hand out any luck candies.

I had one or two friends who supported me without talking behind my back. A couple of rumors related to my status filtered into my ears. One of such rumors particularly hurt me deeply because it originated from close associates. I moved on. I got reports about some of my colleagues who petitioned the Provost to have me expelled on grounds that I was an unmarried expectant mother. The news was both upsetting and surprising. How was it anyone's business what and how I chose to live my life? I overcame the "pull her down syndrome" and ironically, I was never invited to the Dean or Provost's office nor was I served any sort of query. I marched on.

The role of social support

I have seen many people lose focus because of obstacles put in their way by the very persons who should have constituted their support system. In public and clinical health practice, the need for a strong support system for human adaptation or behavioral change is strongly recognized and advocated. To achieve any required behavioral change as a desired outcome, the social support network is always an important first consideration. For instance, to get an illiterate woman to routinely attend prenatal clinics, one would be interested in the practices of her social support network. Do her friends believe prenatal care useful in reaching a desirable maternal-child health outcome? What do her sisters, mother, mother-in-law and grandmother believe and advocate? These are probably her closest allies and the best avenue for influencing her choices. The social support network is often exploited in public health practice to promote good health. Peer groups also constitute a support network.

Amongst teenagers, it is easy to tell the influence of a group of friends on another. Choices or decisions made and perpetrated by our support system often constitute norms and directly or indirectly control our own choices. In every aspect of life, the support network of any individual, especially women, cannot be overlooked. A good support network is integral for survival even in desperate settings. This is the reason breast cancer patients for instance, have support groups; for survivors to instill in others the strength to fight; or for victims to share their struggles and find strength in unity. Generally, in medical and public health practice, a strong social support network is advocated because of its mental and other health benefits. Knowing you're surrounded with supportive people gives you the boost to keep pressing to attain your goals. It improves your sense of belonging, self worth and feeling of security.

In my case, I had no real support system. My family was unaware of my status and even though I had a close relationship with my siblings, I didn't get any support because they were not in the know. I was too scared to let my mother, who happened to be a Deaconess in a strict Pentecostal Church, know I was pregnant. I was sure my father would practically kill me. I was receiving negative vibes from my colleagues at school; my relationship had become unstable at this point and I was all broken inside. I couldn't break the only thing I had going: my will to succeed and put the fifth year of Medical school behind me.

I knew for certain that my strict family would raise so much dust if they knew I was pregnant that I could lose concentration or alter my mental state. My family was dear to me like that. I loved them enough to fear that any disappointment they felt from learning of my condition would irretrievably break me down. So I did what I considered best. It was the wrong choice, especially because I am an African child. But I did what I had to do; I streamlined my focus. I was willing to do whatever I could, within my lawful rights, to reach my goals.

"The difference between a successful person and others is not a lack of strength, not a lack of knowledge, but rather a lack of will." - Vincent T. Lombardi

There is the adage, *"the way you make your bed is how you lie on it."* It was very apt in my case. Since none of my family members knew my emotional, mental and biological state, my support system was restricted. I had no one to hold my hand when I was got so weak and lost immense weight from hyperemesis. I suffered gastritis with Mallory Weiss tears. It progressed to severe gastric ulcer and I had to be stabilized with intravenous anti-ulcer medication. There was no one to make me eat or talk me into staying strong. It was largely my doing but my choices were borne out of the need to succeed. I could have shut down at any one point. I could have taken a sick leave from school. Truth is, I was having none of it. I had defined success as graduating with the MBBS degree along with my class in 2008. I wasn't willing to back down. And so I had to stay focused.

You're probably wondering; *"how did she do? Did she pass her fifth year finals? Did she get in any trouble?"*

Although I didn't care much about it, I was aware there were people who were waiting for me to fail. The timing for the repeat exams (if I failed the first attempt) fell around my expected date of delivery. I had no other choice but to pass on the first try. Otherwise, I would have to repeat the class! If I failed, I'd have to go home and explain it to my dad; he wasn't even aware I was pregnant. I had to pass! There was no other way around it.

The exams were trying. I felt harassed by my examiners during my clinical cases. This was only normal. The examiners often rattled students to assess performance under pressure. You were expected to stay humble through it all. During my pediatric clinical case, I examined a young girl and made a diagnosis of meningitis. The examiner felt it was tetanus. I agreed with him and defended both diagnoses. Meningitis and tetanus infection were differentials, one for the other. The final question I was asked seemed easy but cunning. I was asked to state the commonest pathogen for meningitis in a 12-year old child. If I got it wrong, that was it! I would fail the clinical case. The examiner said as much. I thought for a long minute. I needed to give the answer he wanted to hear.

According to pediatric texts, the commonest causative pathogen for meningitis in children aged five and above is Hemophilus influenza. In clinical practice, especially in the tropics, this wasn't absolutely true. I stood staring at him for a painful moment, weighing my options, before I took the plunge; my answer was *"Streptococcus pneumoniae."* His response gave me hope; he was impressed and accepted my answer. Clinically, in the tropics, particularly Southern Nigeria, S. pneumoniae is the commonest implicated pathogen for meningitis in children aged five and above. If I'd chosen to go with the texts, your guess is as good as mine!

My short clinical cases drew even more criticism. By the time I was done with the clinical cases, I was so upset I wanted to leave without attempting the oral exams, which were just a couple of hours away. I stepped away from my colleagues and wept in frustration and fear. The tears flowed for a while. When I was done, I joined up with my classmates again and waited my turn for the orals exams. A few of my colleagues, who were also top of the class, appeared as rattled as I was; perhaps, even worse.

To answer the question above, yes I passed my finals, on the first try. The moment I learned of my success was one of the happiest in my life.

I was well on my way to becoming a Medical doctor.

Backbone

While my style of writing veils the bleakness of the situation I was confronted with, the truth is, I had several concrete measures in place to help me succeed. Contrary to popular opinion among my colleagues, I have never felt exceptionally brilliant. I did have high IQ scores but I never felt special or any kind of way. I just know that I never professed Medicine as a difficult course to study. I saw it as conquerable and the MBBS, achievable. As I look back, it feels like it was a walk in the park, considering my circumstances.

Determination wasn't always my forte. I didn't always have the intense drive to succeed or excel. Did I always want to make an impact? Yes I did. Was I tough enough to see it through? Without thinking, the answer is no! I grew up shy and extremely introverted. I was a type B personality but on the downside I wasn't always comfortable in my skin. I had so many insecurities. And to hide them, I sneaked into a well-constructed shell. I was one inch short of indulging in imaginary friendships. But as the years passed, I transformed. The drive to succeed became more intense within me. I groomed myself and fought for what I wanted so bad that in my yearbook at the end of medical school, I was described as "very determined" by my colleagues. They had seen and watched me go through some extenuating circumstances but still have my head up. What they didn't know were the other demons I had to fight in the dark, when no one else was watching or awake. And there were lots of demons to fight, tons of them! But I sailed through anyway. I accomplished the goal and moved one step toward achieving my dream.

As a teenager, I did not have many friends. As a matter of fact, I have never had many friends. This doesn't bother me much but there have been the few odd minutes when I wished my social network were a little wider than I had allowed it to be. The time often passed and I remained comfortable with my small circle. The most striking thing I remember about my teenage days was my moods. I suffered intense mood swings.

There were days I would *zone out* for no reason and be engulfed in an acute wave of sadness. On such days, I retreated into my shell, performing my chores but barely speaking to anyone. I had siblings who could pull any one out of *a cave* but it never worked with me, not until that wave passed and I was ready to be happy again. It was a cycle that was caused by a feeling of rejection. I love contact and constant affirmation but my parents are typical Africans. They didn't have the time to stop and utter the *"I love yous"* or give hugs. They were busy and besides it wasn't the norm. Unfortunately, I was that child that needed reassurance and hugs. I never got any. So, I grew up with a void; a huge one that I attempted to fill with wanting and having a baby.

Another problem I had as a young girl was low self-esteem. No one who knows me now is really going to believe I suffered from low self-esteem. But I did.

In my mid-teens, I wanted to be a model but I wasn't tall enough. My height haunted me for a very long time. I felt totally inadequate near taller females. I desperately wanted to be tall. My next battle was my facial appearance. I was smart enough to know that pretty people were better appreciated but dumb enough to consider myself ugly. I did everything I could to take care of myself but there was just no contentment. I wanted to be prettier, to be lighter in complexion, to be anything but how I looked. There were the good days I felt I appeared reasonably presentable but sadly there were fewer of such days in a year than there are in a week.

In the midst of all my insecurities, I found solace in writing. Writing was my first recognized hobby. I started on a couple of novels but never finished any. Publishing a book was not a goal I desperately wanted to accomplish. I was content with logging my daily experiences, writing poems and making up stories. I wrote several articles that never made it to a publishing house. I sincerely believe this happened because I never focused on achieving anything through writing. This changed later in life but I missed out on many good opportunities because of my lack of resolution in this area. I was simply not determined.

I have gone around in circles to explain the outcomes for the presence or absence of determination. A determined person is single-minded in purpose. He is not wishy-washy or easily swayed. Circumstances may delay the accomplishment of his goals, but success is certain. Why? Because that is what he has set in his heart to achieve. He sleeps it, eats it, thinks it, dreams it, sees it and speaks it! All of this, he does without consciousness. It is a natural process that occurs once a man sets his heart on a goal and is disciplined enough to go in pursuit. It is the same thing that makes an unknown politician run and win an election as President of his country, the same factor that causes a man to go after a woman he loves or is attracted to whether they belong in same social caste or not. In crude terms, it is what gives you strength to sit through a painful hair-fixing session at the salon when you could just easily walk away. You are determined to look beautiful.

Life is filled with challenges and I am yet to see any legend, living or dead, who was/is spineless. The wealthiest or most talked about men today are those whose creativity came to light through determination. You're free to reel out the names of wealthy people who had their wealth bequeathed to them and never had to work a day in their lives. We can compare lists when you're done because I have a book full of such persons. So take your moment, make your list. How many of these men have their footprints in the sands of time? How many of these women do you want your daughters to emulate? How many of them die fulfilled?

Ideas can be forgotten or lost in the abstract realm if fear of failure prevails. John C. Maxwell aptly states, *"When you're losing, everything hurts."* But He also agrees that if you fear to lose, you miss the chance to learn. Through determination, life's battles are worn. Remember Joshua, the Bible's warrior? One of my most loved stories about him was when he asked the *"sun to stand still"* (Joshua 10: 12 &13). He was determined to win the war and wasn't taking chances on nightfall. And yes, the sun obeyed his command and he finished the fight in victory. It is the same with our struggles. Obstacles fade in oblivion when we set our eyes on a prize and go after it wholeheartedly. Multiple award-winning artiste, R. Kelly, was not far from the truth when he sang *"if you can see it, then you can be it."*

Determination is not in-born; neither can it be purchased with money. Determination requires discipline. It is a sacrificial process and can be cultivated stepwise. There is the saying, *"you don't know how strong you are, until being strong is the only option you have."* This is the summary of my successes. Not one thing has come easy but every success, every milestone, has been worth the struggle.

Determination is a positive emotion; it is the motivation that pushes you to work towards achieving a certain goal. Determination breeds perseverance. If you have ever persevered and missed your goal anyway, do not fret. The lessons you learnt cannot be dismissed; they will come in handy when the occasion arises. Perseverance through challenges with resultant success sets us up to achieve greater goals. As long as there is life, there will always be more heights to conquer, more grounds to cover, more glory to attain.

I hope that recounting my experiences and the principles that helped me succeed helps any woman, any person, undergoing stress or extremely challenging situations. I hope that you can learn, practice, and find strength within yourself to overcome your struggle.

I am not a very good storyteller, so I may not appeal to your senses or do some of those wonderful things authors do to stir up emotions within you. I only intend to share my struggles and the principles that helped me succeed where others may have backed away. My sincere desire is to stir your mind, to draw up strength in you so that you may live your dream.

Make no mistake; determination is key to achieving success.

Illustration Format: Determination

iFormat 2

Case one

Mya was on the fast track to success. She was from a wealthy home and has had a solid support structure from birth. She had good connections, resources and means. She faced every obstacle squarely and often succeeded at whatever she did. Sadly, she recently broke down and was diagnosed with exhaustion.

Case Two

Logan is preparing for his dissertation presentation. He has worked hard the past four years to complete the requirements for his doctoral degree. He is currently ahead of his classmates because from the first day of the program he began working towards the final day. He always ensured every test or assignment was turned in at the right time. As the day for final dissertation draws closer, unlike some of his colleagues who are frantic, Logan appears balanced and in control.

Case Three

Ashley is an entrepreneur. She went into business believing her ideas were the next big thing. She created many good products but her intense marketing efforts didn't always yield the right results. Instead of being frustrated when she was faced with a loss, Ashley would move her target a little lower to create an illusion of success. Once, her very supportive father offered to buy most of the products she had for sale so she wouldn't suffer loss and she happily accepted. Although she is still interested in her business and believes in the uniqueness and quality of her products, she accepts success as dynamic, depending on a momentary outcome. She hopes she to break out someday but is presently content with adjusting her goals to meet her achievements.

Case Analysis and solution

We often find ourselves in one or more of the scenarios described above. Some of us may not be from a wealthy family but we have or are experiencing Mya's pain. We face every challenge head on without taking time to be deliberate. While the "succeed at all cost" mentality is advantageous, it is important to learn to apply it with a sense of direction. It is rewarding to squarely face certain problems and achieve immediate results but a successful career cannot be achieved this way. It has to be worked for, like Logan did, with deliberation, sacrifice and direction. Some of the days Logan refused to party or go out on social meetings, he was navigating himself towards his definition of success. He paid a price but ultimately he is reaching his goal almost effortlessly. Unlike Ashley, he isn't about to turn in an incomplete or incoherent work. He isn't about to extend his dissertation for another year because he actually could if he so desired. Early on, He defined his goal and created a clear vision of what success entailed for him and put a timeline to it. Unlike Mya, he isn't exhausted or risking losing it all; and contrary to Samira, he isn't redefining success; he is sticking to the plan.

Notes

Coastal determination exacts less on the mind and directs an individual steadily towards a defined goal. It requires sacrifice, diligence and discipline but in the end you will have your dream in sight. Uphill determination, that is pressing on against all seeming barriers is only advocated for short term challenges, as it will invariably burn you out. It is better to apply a calculated approach to success and only occasionally infuse the "win at all costs" attitude to overcome temporary issues. Also, remember, accepting the easy way out to reach your goal isn't exactly success; it may just be an illusion. If you want to be a billionaire, don't settle for millionaire, and say I'm wealthy anyway. Go for it!

CHAPTER THREE
THE POWER OF VISION

The most important feature in a creative person is vision. Every successful man had or has a vision. Without vision, determination is pointless. What would you be focused on if you had nothing you intended to accomplish?

What is that one thing that your heart desires? People often think that vision is timeless. They believe as long as you have breath in your lungs, you can fulfill and achieve your vision. This is wrong, so wrong. If your vision is not time bound then there is no goal. And if there is no goal, why have a vision?

"For the vision is yet for the appointed time; It hastens toward the goal and it will not fail." (Habakkuk 2:3)

According to Pastor Myles Munroe, *"Vision is a source of hope; it's the source of courage; it's the source of perseverance in the midst of difficulty."*

At some point, during my time at Hopkins, I put up the following post on my Facebook.

"When you know where you're going, it's easier to tackle the challenges that appear in your path. When you can see your goal, it's easy to see obstacles as the mere props that they are.

R. Kelly's "if you can see it, then you can be it," comes to mind. There's a reason I don't break; it's not because I'm so strong; it's because I have seen the end from the beginning, so I focus on getting there. God's word says, "Better is the end of a matter than the beginning."

When I said, "see your goal," like many other authors, I wasn't referring to "seeing with the physical eyes" but with the *mind's eye.* If you can figure out what you want your end (goal/purpose) to be, then you won't let challenges faze you. You will keep walking towards it. I carry a very vivid vision inside of me. It's the reason I gave up my desire to become a plastic surgeon for public health. I remember my colleagues and superiors in clinical practice expressing their disappointment when I announced I was quitting clinical practice. I don't mean to be proud; but I was a very good clinician. My patients always ended up loving me and in most cases would ask to see me whenever they returned to the hospital where I practiced.

The medical director at the hospital where I worked wanted me to be a pediatrician or pediatric surgeon. I understood why. Above all, I loved clinical practice. It gave me a sense of satisfaction and service. Granted, the wages didn't always pay the bills but I was cool. However, I didn't want to be trapped in a routine. I didn't want to wait in the clinic while disasters were happening all around me. I wanted to be proactive and be able to give help where I felt it mattered most. So, I chose public health. Oh! Make no mistake, I sometimes long for the securities that clinical practice offers, in place of the uncertainties of a public health career; but I carry my vision inside of me. It's so vivid; in times when clouds threaten it, all I do is replay a certain picture and I'm fired up again. That picture is associated with the success of my vision and it drives me to focus and succeed. Someday soon, the picture will become reality.

When God made man, He put in him everything to succeed. How do I know this?

"And God blessed them, and God said unto them, Be fruitful, and multiply, and replenish the earth, and subdue it: and have dominion over the fish of the sea, and over the fowl of the air, and over every living thing that moveth upon the earth." (Genesis 1:28)

"For God has already given you everything you need." (1Corinthians 3:21b; TLB)

As Dr. Myles Munroe put it, *"You are your best raw material."* No excuse is good enough to not have a vision; unless you're content walking through life as a nobody, believing in your heart that the men who succeed are made of better stuff than you. However, neither thinking nor believing it will make it true. You owe it to yourself to succeed in life, at what you do; in your relationships and marriage or whatever else it is that matters to you. Don't blame your lack of vision or *"failure on your lack of funds, friendships or connections. You can't even blame it on lack of ideas; no one was born a failure."* -Myles Munroe

Vision meets determination

For me, an unwedded pregnant fifth year medical student, my vision was to become a doctor. However, to get to that point I had to accomplish several goals. I had numerous continuous assessment tests to take and pass but the ultimate goal for that level was to pass my third professional MBBS exams. This was the gateway to the 6th or final year and ultimately becoming a doctor. At this point in my life, everything was bleak. Success seemed far; so very far. It wasn't just that I was pregnant; it was more that I was going through an extremely difficult pregnancy. As doctors or the web reveal, women suffering from hyperemesis gravidarum often need to stay in bed. In severe cases, intravenous fluids are infused to maintain blood glucose levels and correct electrolyte imbalances. I had a bad case requiring several hospital admissions and bed rests at home. On school mornings, the infusion lines had to come off so I could join my class during ward rounds. On one occasion, I went straight to clinical rounds with the infusion cannula still in my hand. The worst part was the complication of protracted vomiting. I had retched hard enough to have gastric tears, causing me to vomit frank blood. This happened repeatedly and at one time, I was marked up for transfusion. Thankfully, I wasn't transfused.

My number one mentor is Ben Carson. His story touches my heart deeply and his success is more than worthy of emulation. His books, "Gifted Hands" and the "Think Big" changed my life immensely. I believe, "Gifted Hands" broke the chain of mediocrity in my life. I read it as a teenager and my thought process was revolutionized. Ben Carson put the Johns Hopkins University on the map for me and I willed within me to study at this world-class school.

Prof. Carson is world's most renowned Pediatric neurosurgeon. He has conquered more heights in medicine than an artist would dare paint on a canvas. His imagination is more than charming. It is practical and groundbreaking. Ben Carson showed the world what it found difficult to comprehend through his proficiency in neurosurgery. The first intra-uterine surgeries on fetus are credited to him, rewriting medical texts in the process. He is famous for separating conjoined twins, being the first to successfully do so at the head. According to reports from the Johns Hopkins Hospital, Dr. Carson is a specialist in traumatic brain injuries, brain and spinal cord tumors, achondroplasia, neurological and congenital disorders, craniosynostosis, epilepsy, and trigeminal neuralgia. Wow!

Dr. Carson has extremely high "hand-eye coordination" which accorded him the "gifted surgeon title."

The amazing thing is, Dr. Carson, was raised singly by his mother, Sonya who dropped out of school in third grade and married at 13! Sonya divorced her husband and raised her two sons, Ben and his brother, Curtis alone. His biography states his mother often took on two or more jobs, mostly as a domestic servant, to cater for her sons.

Despite her obvious challenges, Sonya wasn't going to let her sons future go to ruin or be inconsequential for that matter. She is recorded as a tough determined woman who instilled in her son the desire to succeed. Ms. Sonya cut her sons' TV time and made them study daily, having them turn in weekly reports that she could barely read. But they didn't know that.

As a young man, Ben did get in trouble many times. He almost hit his mother with a hammer because she disputed his choice of clothes. He reportedly stabbed his friend during a disagreement but fortunately the knife blade broke on the victim's belt buckle. Regardless of these incidents, Ben matured to become a responsible man. Today, he is one of the most gifted surgeons, certainly the most gifted in recent history; equaled only, perhaps by Derek Sheppard of the Grey's anatomy series!

Dr. Carson is well on his way to becoming America's next President.

The lesson to learn here is not only of Prof Carson's success but of his mother's strong will. Ms. Sonya was limited in a way that could have stunted her children's growth. She only got as far as third grade in elementary school. She married at 13! To make matters worse, she got divorced and had to fend for and raise her sons all by herself. She was dogged by sufficient reasons to keep her children mediocre. She could have been a careless, nonchalant mother. I salute her courage, her drive, and backbone. She is one super mom!

For every one reading this, who is impressed with her or her son's achievements, I want you to know it's easy to find a crevice to hide and "un-relate" her frustrations. She lives in America; there is a welfare system; the schools are great; and so on. I just want you to know, failure has many excuses.

While I have maintained that will power is not innate, its learning begins early and often in paths that are less than desirable. The desire to succeed may begin at any point in our lifetime. It is then up to us to nurture it to fruition.

At every phase in life, we are faced with various hurdles. Our worth at any point will predict how much energy we exert to reach success. For instance, a financially proficient man exerts less mental activity or physical energies in overcoming a financial challenge. In same way, a man learned or skilled in computer programming finds it easier to create a meaningful application than a beginner. However, for each one of these men, the desire to succeed at each goal is what keeps him till it is achieved.

There is no flawless individual in this world. There are only those who don't let their flaws stop them; who don't let their mistakes hold them back. Take Dr. Carson's mom for instance, she dropped out in third grade! Did that stop her from wanting an education for her kids or directing her son on to the paths of greatness? No! Determination does not see flaw as an enemy. It embraces flaws and recognizes it as a distraction that is insignificant and conquerable in the path to success.

You're probably saying to yourself, *"but I am not that strong; stuff weighs me down easily and I can't keep fighting."* Or maybe you even feel, *"I have tried so hard and it's just not working, I can't keep at this."* I almost smile at this because I have felt every kind of way there is to make me bow to discouragement. I have felt so despondent that I wanted to die. But guess what? Yielding to fears and frustrations is cowardly and totally irresponsible. If ever you want to succeed, keep hoping, keep confessing, develop a strong will; it pays.

Steps to nurturing determination and vision
1. What is your vision?
You cannot be determined without a vision. You cannot have success if you do not have a goal.

You cannot be determined without a vision. You cannot have success if you do not have a goal.

Google defines vision as the "faculty or state of being able to see." Period! Dreams are different from vision, even though some people mix them up. Dreams are ideas, images, sensations or emotions created in our imagination. They exist only in our minds. But a vision has been drawn from the mind to sight. A vision can be built from a dream. In fact a dream becomes a vision when a man takes steps or performs actions aimed at making it reality. When a tech personnel wakes up from a dream/imagination in which he saw himself building a revolutionary mobile application and then seeks the resources to recreate the picture, he's on his way to building his vision. When you stop wishing to start a business and sit down to draw up a business plan, no matter how crude it may turn out, you're beginning a vision.

As a child, I heard about R.G Letourneau, without ever knowing his name. We were taught in Church about a very wealthy man who gave 90% of his income to God and kept 10% for himself. Robert Gilmore Letourneau was an American businessman born in the 19th century into a Christian family. He dropped out of school at the age of 14 and encountered many hurdles on the way to finding his vision. As he grew, he developed an interest in automobiles and sought to gain as much knowledge as he could in the field. He went through several jobs as a farm hand, bricklayer, miner, woodcutter, and participated in the construction of a bridge, developing in the process, a desire to utilize his acquired skills. After many years of experience in various mechanical trades and labor, Letourneau settled to design his own earth moving machinery.

He is largely credited with the invention of most of the earth moving machineries being used today, having held more than 300 patents and possessed machinery plants in four continents. During the Second World War, he supplied 70% of all heavy earth moving equipment used by the Allied Forces (now United Nations). Despite being ahead of his generation in machinery invention, Mr. Letourneau's keen mind saw a future for machineries that was far beyond his current inventions. He had a vision of machines whose abilities and capacities transcended what was obtainable, even with his inventions. His descriptions clearly described the future of machineries. His life is a demonstration of the power of vision regardless of circumstance. Long after his death, his accomplishments inspire us to believe that any man can be a success and celebrated expert in any chosen field if he develops a keen vision.

2. Work on your internal integrity

As humans, we all have differing levels of capacities and internal integrities.

Our capacity is largely influenced by external factors such as our level of education, and the political, social, economic and religious environment to which we are exposed. Oftentimes, these environments may limit us and distort our creative prowess. Internal integrity refers to our innate abilities, and in this context, infers the drive to succeed. A person with high internal integrity will overcome seeming insurmountable barriers to reach success. This is the reason why a man can drop out of Harvard University but still turn out to be the wealthiest person alive. It is also why a tailor with no training in the oil and gas sector can become one of the world's wealthiest women.

Pakistani activist, Malala Yousafzai is a great example of someone with high internal integrity. Her level of education, political and religious backgrounds were barriers that she broke through her internal integrity to become the youngest Nobel peace prize recipient in history. Through self-determination, she pressed on with her women and human rights campaign, even in the face of death. She had a vision; to see women receive education, and she motivated herself to work towards it. Born in 1997 in Pakistan, Malala was fortunate to have parents who believed in educating female children. Her family ran a chain of schools in a region where the Taliban had repeatedly banned females from going to school. At ages 11-12, Malala blogged for the BBC, chronicling her life under the Taliban who were beginning to gain control of her town. As she aged, Malala grew more vocal in her beliefs and fight for women's education. This irked the Taliban who orchestrated an assassination plot against her in 2012. Although she received a near fatal bullet wound to her head during the attack, Malala survived.

Her story began a revolution that saw the Pakistani Government endorse the first "Right to Education" bill. She was named one of 100 most influential people in the world in 2013, and has won several awards including, a honorary doctoral degree from University of Kings College in Halifax, honorary Canadian citizenship, the Sakharov prize, the first Pakistani National Youth Peace prize and the Nobel Peace prize which she shared with Kailash Satyarthi from India. Malala may not be a mother but she is one superwoman! She may not have the brawn for Pakistani politics but she developed herself to become a respected voice in human rights activism.

Not many people know that Asa Candler, the founder of the Coca Cola Company was born into a very humble family or that he was initially a drug store clerk. Starting from humble beginnings, Asa Candler built the Coca Cola brand after purchasing its patent from the original owner. Although he was not educationally qualified, Candler developed aggressive innovative methods for the advertisement and distribution of his product, beginning the foundation for one of the world's largest empires today. Looking at the Coca Cola brand, it is almost impossible to imagine its humble roots; it is almost impossible to believe that it was founded and marketed by someone who had absolutely no training in the sector. Asa Candler developed himself by working on his internal integrity.

John D. Rockefeller, described as the world's greatest businessman, was born to a Christian mother and a father who's best described as unscrupulous. Despite the negative examples set by his father, John D. Rockefeller decided to become self-reliant, developing himself and seeking education. Armed with a sharp business acumen and determination, he overcame numerous obstacles, and proceeded to float his own company, Standard Oil. By innovating and initiating his own ideas, he built his business into a massive conglomerate that was very beneficial to investors. He ensured that every angle, through which he could monopolize the oil market back in the day, was covered. He integrated production, marketing, and distribution to control thirty percent of the oil market. Mr. Rockefeller was once the world's wealthiest man and the first American to become a billionaire. However, the root of his success is deep in the development of his internal abilities. John D. refused to be limited by his familial circumstances and went on to be recorded in history. He was an ordinary man who was able to do extraordinary things because he worked on his personal integrity.

The man, Tyler Perry, is perhaps one of the best breakout stories to which any one going through extenuating circumstances can best identify. As I follow his story, I often wonder to myself why I did not start sooner. Tyler is a clear example that anyone can become "someone" if they develop themselves from within. He was raised by an abusive father who later turned out not to have any biological ties with him.

As a child, Tyler was a victim of sexual molestation and he once contemplated suicide. His mother took him to Church weekly, a place where he admittedly found some solace. Although he did not finish high school, he earned his diploma and developed himself to write. He wrote materials related to his personal experiences and graduated to theatre production and film partnerships. Today, Tyler Perry is one of the most respected names in the film industry, with a net worth of $400million. Though he was once homeless, he can now afford any house of his dreams. He is a sterling example of what a man can accomplish through self-development.

3. Be consistent

You cannot ask God for tuition when you sit at home doing nothing. You cannot ask God for a shop/office when you can begin a mobile service. Bring faith alive by your works. Every time I went to class when my tuition was yet to be paid, it was a struggle. To get out of bed, get my kids and I ready, and then walk to the bus stop to get to school and attend classes knowing I couldn't even afford the bus fare wasn't easy. There were mornings that I didn't want to get out of bed. I hadn't paid tuition; I didn't have the $1.60 fare to get on the bus! While some drivers understood once I explained I didn't have the money, others were downright mean. I didn't blame them. It was my duty to pay my fare but I couldn't afford it. I was embarrassed most times, but the next morning I'd repeat the same action all over again. I had to get to school.

Once I had to psych myself to keep going by repeatedly asking, *"How will God pay the fees if I stay home?"* Even though it was the most humbling to do, I had to keep at it. I had to be consistent even when I got a message from the program office to stop attending classes. When it neared the end of term and I wasn't still registered, I didn't stop. I didn't dare. Course registration officially closed but I still showed up at classes. And yes, the miracle came through.

Sometimes, being consistent in maintaining vision is the toughest thing to do. You know, maybe nothing is working, the funds are not coming in, business is failing, your boss is being mean, you're getting more losses than profits; the list goes on. I enjoin you, keep at it. This is not to uphold consistence in foolhardiness but to encourage persistence to achieve a goal. In order to succeed, it is important to hold a pertinent vision. Your vision will undergo refinements, modifications, additions and some subtractions as time passes but you must maintain consistency in purpose.

When Tyler's first production, *"I Know I've Been Changed,"* hit the theatre in 1990, it received poor reviews and was a financial failure. He had invested his $12,000 life-savings in it and must have felt like a failure. I mean, this was a young man struggling to overcome the odds of his childhood and his entire investment seemed like it just went down the drain!

Many of us give up at points like this one. We fail to understand that life is filled with challenges but we must keep pressing to reach our goals. Not Tyler!

Over the ensuing years, he re-wrote the stage production, modifying it and learning in the process. He designed new stage shows and was consistently on the road to showcase his productions. By 2005, he had sold over a $150million in tickets, videos and merchandise. Tyler brings new life to the meaning of persistence. I dread to imagine his outcome if he had let people's opinions or his early financial failures deter him. Here is a man with a vision, who developed and honed his skill and remained consistent. He reached his prize despite the odds stacked against him. Today, an estimated live audience of at least 35,000 persons attends his shows weekly.

Winners don't quit.

The Technicalities of vision

During the third term of my MPH program, I took a course I had been looking forward to, "Managing Non Governmental Organizations in the Health Sector." As it turned out, the class was completely worth it. On my first day of class, I was introduced to the book, "The Fifth Discipline", by author Peter M. Senge. The book literally turned my thinking inside out, in a good way. It is a "must read" for anyone who aspires to be successful. I had the opportunity to review this book for my final paper and some of the teachings continue to inspire me long after the end of class.

A conceived vision is idealistically different from present reality, such that huge disparities may exist between both. Say for instance, your vision is to become a successful writer but the reality is that you're not educated. The gap between that vision (to become a successful writer) and current reality (lack of education) is called creative tension. This is very different from emotional tension and is capable of spelling doom for any vision. For the illustration above, there are two options. The first option is to pull up reality to meet the vision (become educated); or pull down the vision to meet reality (you're not educated; you can't be a writer; forego or lower your vision).

Notably, there are many other factors that may constitute challenges or serve as distractions to the realization of this vision, such as lack of funds for tuition, your age and other factors beyond your control. However, the reality remains the same, you're not literate. Let's assume you wanted to be an inspirational writer or even a novelist. After considering your *creative tension* you may decide to take the minimum adult education classes and settle for writing books for kindergarten children. You will still become a writer but you have lowered your vision. Successful people are those who are able to sustain creative tension and pull reality to meet their vision. They get educated to the highest level required (if that's what it takes) to help them succeed; they take on part time jobs to help with funding; they march on even in the face of uncontrollable obstacles to achieve their goals. These are the people who become creative because they break all barriers to succeed, setting new records in the process.

Creativity requires persistence and the ability to sustain your vision in the midst of countless odds. Steve Jobs faced several hurdles before he could turn Apple Inc. to what it is today. During his tenure as the company's CEO, the company registered success, so much so that he turned the near-bankrupt Apple Inc. to a profitable company within two years. He had a vision, that personal computers would revolutionize lifestyle, entertainment, and educational models. He was said to have envisioned a world wide Internet in 1985. It all didn't come cheaply; he faced challenges. He left Apple Inc. in 1985 after almost a decade of working with his cofounder, Steve Wozniack. When he left as a result of disagreement with the board of directors, he must have felt wasted and at a loss. He must have felt like his dream was slipping through his fingers. After leaving Apple, he kept at it; founding and getting involved in other tech companies.

In 1996, about a decade after he left, Steve Jobs returned to Apple. This time, the company needed him more than he needed it; he returned and made history with Apple Inc. Today, the apple OS, designed by Steve Job's interim company, NeXT Inc., is the commonest operating system in the world. His revolutionary iPhone and iPad set the standard for competitor's products. Steve's story was not an easy one. He was an adopted child and a college dropout. But his life was one of dedication and consistence of purpose. He had a vision; he worked and walked towards it. Despite challenges, he remained focused and pulled up reality to meet his vision until his vision became the reality. When Steve Jobs passed on in 2011, the world paid attention and mourned like he was a superhero. If you ask me, he was.

There are many leading examples of men who have successfully revolutionized the world because they stuck to their guns. Some picked a few ideas here and there and modified them into their vision. Every time, I think about Bill Gates and Mark Zuckerberg, I know I can't fail. I take solace in knowing they were made of the same substance as I was and we were all given the same directive to go "prosper." I know there's someone reading this book that is about to give up on their marriage, their job and whatever it is they hold dear to their hearts. Listen to me, the very fact that you're frustrated means you care, if you didn't, you would shrug it off. I say to you, don't give up. You can't give up. On the inside of you, resides a champion. You need to let him come to the surface. It may take you a little time to get to the end but keep fighting.

Think of Mohammed Ali. He fought till he called himself "the greatest." Until you can say that about yourself, I mean honestly assess and can confidently utter those words about yourself, you don't get to give up. Someone's future may depend on that very business you're about to give up on. A whole nation's survival may be dependent on that technology that is causing you nightmares. Whatever it is you have envisioned in the past, keep at it; don't lose it. Keep seeing it, start saying it; don't stop praying it. Only then will the universe yield and give you that which you seek.

I mentioned earlier, that I hold a vision close to my heart.

Very few people know it. Maybe one or two persons but the pictures I have painted on my mind from that vision keep me going. Every time I want to switch careers or just do something different because this "isn't working" I remember these pictures and I keep at it. It was those mental pictures that got me out of bed and on the bus to school when I couldn't figure out how to tell the drivers I had no fare. It was those pictures that made me go without food for days yet stay focused.

These same pictures kept me going to school without missing a course when I fell down the stairs and broke my leg in the middle of my MPH program. On top of barely having money to feed, I now had a broken leg, a sprained ankle on the other leg, a 12-week old baby, rent issues plus tedious coursework from school. I didn't stop. I kept going. My hair was cut short, unkempt; I didn't have any good clothes. On good days I looked like a homeless beggar, and I am not exaggerating. When my mom came visiting after I broke my leg, she wept when she saw me. But still I kept it moving. And that's why I enjoin you to keep moving. In the end, I got my degree. I'm on track, walking towards the accomplishment of the big picture. If I could do it with all of the distractions and mental tussle I have been through, you can do it too.

Don't wait for money or sweat the absence of determined genes, begin cultivating your will power today. I am excited at the thought of the potential that is about to come alive in you. I see you follow in the paths of these ordinary men who refused to stay mediocre but applied themselves till they became extraordinary. I know it's in you. As I write this book, I develop a new mantra, *"let nothing stop you."*

Illustration Format: The Power of Vision

iFormat 3

Ethan has just turned forty but instead of celebrating, he is broken. He has been in the construction business for decades, slowly working his way up from a brick layer to the managerial position which he currently occupies; at least as of two days ago. He has just turned in his resignation but is unsure where to begin again. While he has invested his time in his work, he had been deeply conscious of his lack of satisfaction and fulfillment. As a little boy, Ethan dreamt of owning Estates, refurbishing and selling them to make more money. Now at 40, he can no longer grasp the bits of his childhood dream. He is now out of a job and beginning to develop anxiety symptoms because of his predicament.

Application

Not everyone is in Ethan's exact situation but the scenario doesn't sound strange. You may not have resigned from your current job or even had a job for that matter but feel a deep sense of dissatisfaction with what you're currently doing. You my have become disillusioned with your life and dreams but the only thing worse than failing is not trying at all. If certain attributes of this case appear similar to your situation, it is okay to take some time out, think and apply several of the principles you find in this book.

Analysis

1. Take some time out to empty your head. For instance take a 24hour break for work. I would do this on Friday to take advantage and have a long weekend. You are encouraged to sleep all day Friday but once night falls, get your workbook out and start work.

2. What's important to you? Is it fulfillment or security. Bear in mind that this may the most important question you will ever have to answer and your response will largely determine the outcome of your life henceforth.

3. Write down your answer. If you chose security, I completely understand and you need to know there is no foolish choice. It's win-win but also know there's a bigger win. If you chose fulfillment, I say congratulations. You have just unlocked the door to your internal potential. Proceed to subsequent help lines.

4. List two major plans things that will make you feel fulfilled when achieved.

5. Which is the more important plan? Which of these two will cause you to look back at age eighty and smile knowing you lived your life to the fullest? Write it down. Don't be afraid to

dream or come up with lofty ideas. It just has to be what matters to you.

6. Now we have a single plan. What do you see? How far do you want this idea to take you? What do you hope to achieve with your idea? Do you want to bring up a new product? Is it a service? Whatever it is, write it down. This is your vision.

7. Today, you're at reality, but you won't be here forever. It's time to begin pulling reality up to meet your vision and make your vision reality. To achieve this, you need to think and do some research. How can you achieve your dream? Write down what you find on a fresh page. For instance, if your vision is to have your own cosmetic line, there are many ways you can achieve this. You can search on the Internet for private label cosmetic companies who can design and manufacture your products or you can take some basic lessons to become your own manufacturer. Be sure to write down your decision on which path to follow to reach your dream.

8. Apply all you have learnt in chapter one and two. Think and confess positively; do not harbor fear and positively declare the word of God. Stay determined to succeed and always keep your eyes on your goals. Pray.

9. Begin to develop your inner abilities. For instance you may be a natural at mixing colors or innovating new make up

ideas, research more, practice more and be sure to write down whatever ideas or formulas you come up with. These will become useful frameworks to develop your line of business. Don't be limited by your environment or circumstance, always seek other avenues to circumvent an obstacle.

10. Stick with the plan. Many people begin something really good but then "chuck it up" because they do not reap immediate benefits. Don't fall into this group. Resolve to succeed and stay single-minded to your goal. Everyday, think of something new related to your goal and add it to the plan.

11. Write your vision in one sentence on a thin piece of paper and stick on your bathroom mirror or bedroom wall. You want to see it always.

The next chapters will help you gain insight to how you make your vision become a reality.

CHAPTER FOUR
OVERCOMING DISTRACTIONS

A man can have an awesome vision, be self-motivated, with enviable resources and yet still be unable to achieve his vision. This may happen because of challenges not directly related to his project but they cause him to stumble anyway. In the path to fulfilling purpose and reaching our goals, many obstacles may line the way. People lose focus and miss their mark because a loved one died, or they lost their job or took that one more drink that they shouldn't have.

Distractions come in many forms but you must see them for what they are, otherwise you will falter. I grew up thinking obstacles were negative factors intended to stop me from reaching a goal. If you also think this way, you're wrong. To become a success, you must embrace the hurdles in your path. You have to see them as part of the line-up that culminates in success. When you do, you generate less emotional tension and save up energy for chasing your vision. Overcoming distractions may not come as easy as I reel it out but trust me, I have been there and so I can tell you for free, that the hurdles in your way serve to make your testimony of success more amazing. Success is not a smooth ride. The rougher the path, the tougher your ride, and the stronger you become. If you want to be a billionaire, be ready for a billion dollar challenge. Success comes to those who prove themselves, to the last men standing.

For every hurdle you overcome as a person or an entrepreneur, there is a prize. You have just improved your portfolio and increased your resilience. For every time you fail, you learn one more way that does not end in success. The next time you are confronted with a similar challenge, you easily become a victor. According to John C. Maxwell, *"sometimes you lose, sometimes you learn."* And as David Ibiyeomie put it, *"Failure is the opportunity to start more intelligently."*

While some combat external distractions, for many others, the distraction is internal. When I was first told I'd be sent back home without completing my degree at Hopkins, my heart sank. I had many other external distractions. But now I had to deal with fear too. And oh! I was afraid, very afraid. But I dealt with it. I couldn't handle it all alone so I went to God with it.

Handling distractions is often dependent on whether they are internal (mind; fear; worries; despair) or external (habits;

associations; difficulty; needs). Truly, there is no obstacle that cannot be overcome. My number one mantra, also chanted by many across the world, *"impossible is nothing,"* is very apt. When Steve Jobs spoke about the entire world being connected to the Internet in 1985, people must have tagged it impossible. Barely three decades later, his dream is alive.

As someone who has had to handle all sorts of distractions in the pathway to success, I share some of my best steps for moving forward.

1. Work on your mentation

This is one of the most important exercises I indulge in. You may bump into me sometime and hear me mutter under my breath, *"Impossible is nothing."* I say it all the time because I have to remind myself that even though I may not have the connections that some do, I'll excel beyond their best. There is no other choice; I have got to get to the top. If you must overcome, you must constantly work on your mind. Most of the work we need to do to make progress in life is done in our minds. All battle, no matter the significance, is won in the mind.

No king goes to war and prevails when he believes he will lose. He goes, believing against all odds that the battle is his for the taking. This is the overcomer's mentality. As he prepares for battle, he draws up images of a battle plan that will enable him succeed. His eyes are set on the big picture, the prize that comes with success. So, he builds his mind and mentally strategizes. Until he does this, he is unable to lead his army. Same way, you must paint the picture of your vision and brand your soul with it. You must be careful while undertaking this process because the designs of your heart are what you will confess, and what you'll eventually receive. As a writer clearly put it, *"be careful what you fill your thoughts with because ultimately, this is the design your life will follow."*

Dealing with the distractions of the mind depends on what mental struggles you face. As a Christian, seek out scriptural verses that can hold you through worries and fears. Whenever you feel the aura of despair setting in, remind yourself of God's promises. Inspire yourself by reading the biographies of living legends that were embroiled in similar situations. Think of Ben Carson, the dumb school kid that turned out to be the greatest Neurosurgeon in the history of time; think of Steve Jobs the adopted child or of Bill Gates the Harvard dropout, who both revolutionized technology. If these men seem far removed from you or abstract, then think of Malala Yousafzai, the teenage Nobel prize winner who came face to face with death but refused to back down; think of me, the penniless woman with a broken leg, a sprained other ankle, with two kids to cater for but still made it through Hopkins and chasing the big picture.

Like many women in Africa and in fact over the world, I am an avid user of Mary Kay cosmetics. I learnt of Mary Kay Ash's (the founder of Mary Kay cosmetics) inspiring story years ago. I often describe her as a victim of mental models.

Mental models are powerful influences on individual, or organizational outcomes. They influence our mentation and can either limit or set us free. Mental models, which I colloquially refer to as mindsets, are capable of hindering progress in any one area if left unexamined. For instance you may refuse to go along with a partnership, which holds profound benefits for you because you hold a certain belief against the other party.

In an organization, a manager may refuse to work with an employee or vice versa because one perceives the other to be arrogant, unfriendly or unproductive. In reality, this may not be true but personal assumption may have seared a negative impression so deeply on one party's mind that he is set against any relationship even when it is mutually beneficial. This happens all the time. I once lost a school election because people believed I was snobbish and proud when in fact I was introverted and reserved. In fact, I was repeatedly told that despite my qualification for the position and the achievements I could accomplish, my perceived personality could not be ignored.

Mindsets hold a deep stake in success. A man who believes a task cannot be accomplished can never succeed at that task no matter how equipped he becomes. We are capable of limiting ourselves through our beliefs but could also be the victim of another person's mental model. Mary Kay Ash is proof that even in such cases, success and excellence can be achieved. Mary Kay Ash worked for over 10 years in a male-dominated business but resigned when a man she trained was promoted ahead of her. She went on to found Mary Kay cosmetics, setting up a small store in Dallas. Her victimization, stemming from management decisions, which placed men ahead of women turned out to be a blessing.

Instead of lamenting her fate and wasting away, Mary Kay drew up a fresh vision by employing intense mental activity.

She designed a business scheme that was centered on employee reward and her model has been adopted by many organizations worldwide. From a $5,000 investment in her personal cosmetic line, Mary Kay Cosmetics turned in $1million in its first year. Today, the company boasts over 1.6million salespersons worldwide and is worth billions of dollars. Although she has passed on, the legacy she created lives, to bear fruits from which future investors may still reap.

Neither you nor I have any reason to fail; *"impossible is nothing!"*

2. Paint a vivid mental picture

A vision is not in motion until you see it. You may have an idea in your head and something tells you this could be the next big thing. Or maybe you've been working on a project for a while and you've gotten to a deadlock. What picture do you have in your head? Long before Ben Carson started performing surgeries in utero, he had developed a mental picture. When the time came, he was ready. And he made history.

"The Lord said to Abram after Lot had parted from him, "Look around from where you are, to the north and south, to the east

and west. All the land that you see I will give to you and your offspring forever." (Genesis 13:14&15)

"Until you see it, you are not getting it; until you see it, you can't be it. "

In all of the troubles I faced prior to graduation, I had to keep seeing myself in my graduation gown; I had to develop the picture in my head and keep calling it up. This was a short-term goal but I needed it to reach where I am headed. It was vital to my vision. So, I drew a vivid image and branded my mind with it until it came to pass. These mental images are powerful. They have the power to automatically re-focus you from whatever distraction lies in your path and maintain you on the track to success. Use your imagination as a psychological arsenal to achieve your vision but be careful what pictures you paint. Negative pictures will come back to haunt you and break you down but positive pictures will give you hope and remind you of something worth fighting for.

Paul Meyer (1928-2009) described this phenomenon wonderfully. In 1960, Paul J. Meyer founded the Success Motivation Institute (SMI), a self improvement industry that was based on the principle that, *"Whatever you vividly imagine, ardently desire and enthusiastically act upon must inevitably come to pass."* He sincerely believed that all humans could achieve and live a lifetime of success based on this principle and his life proved it.

Paul broke many records in financial and physical fitness history. At 27, he became the youngest member of the Million Dollar Round Table, an association of world-leading life insurance and financial service professionals. He founded and operated over 40 companies and for at least 50years, his personal income ranged between $5-20million per year. As a young boy, Paul received every Boy Scout award that was on offer and he broke physical fitness records in the U.S army, performing more than 3,000 sit-ups at one time.

This was a man who was intense in his belief in the power of mental visualization; excelled through its practice and set out to help others succeed by using it. He founded the Success Motivation Institute (SMI) and sold more than $3billion worth of SMI materials in over 60 countries! That's the power of a vivid mental picture.

3. Surround yourself with men of like passion
When you have a vision, be sure to surround yourself with people of like minds, otherwise they'll take you where they

are going. In the very least, they'll pull you down and what you saw will become blurry and your heart may faint. Worse off, is finding yourself in the company of men without a vision, men who have no aspirations. In the company of such men, you'll become and end as a nonentity; and a nonentity is a failure, to himself, society and mostly, to God.

Tim Ferriss, author and entrepreneur, frightened me with his words, "*The best advice I ever got is: You're the average of the five people you associate with the most.*" When I read this, I felt like I was in trouble. I did a quick mental check to make sure I was with the right crowd. I didn't want to be found wanting because I knew his words were true, oh so true!

After I graduated from medical school, I became friends with one of the persons I went to school with. Previously, I had been very vibrant and focused on where I was headed and only surrounded myself with like-minded persons. I didn't have many friends in school and I talked with very few people. But the few people I mingled with were top of the class, with equal or even more drive than I had. But I got out of school and then got super cozy with someone who was "comfortable in her skin." She didn't want too much out of life but to be married, have kids and land a safe job. Now, there is absolutely nothing wrong with that.

There's nothing wrong with being content, and loving security. But there was a problem. We were opposites. I wanted marriage and kids but I didn't want to be anyone's employee, I wanted to be an employer. She was content; I was hungry. She wanted to be a good doctor; I wanted to revolutionize public health! The relationship didn't last too long but before then, I had gradually come down to her level, becoming content with little and beginning to lower my vision.

Thankfully, I got my groove back! Now, I respect and love her, and she's like a sister to me but I learnt a vital lesson. *"It is much easier for anyone to drag you down than it is for you to pull them up."* You can't desire to move up the ladder of success and keep in the company of men embroiled in your current situation or who are even worse off. And if you're already up, watch your company.

"If you don't know where you're going, any road will get you there."- Lewis Carroll

Because, you will go nowhere!

When I read up on the biographies of some of the men I have exemplified in this book, I found a consistent pattern. They surrounded themselves with men of like mind and passion. Oftentimes, the associations were better and higher placed than they were. As a medical student, Dr. Carson found a mentor in Dr. James Taren, a renowned neurosurgeon; while still in High school, Steve Jobs partnered with Steve Wozniack who was an undergraduate at the University of California, Berkeley; Bill Gates had Paul Allen, his partner and two years his senior. Together, they worked for success.

One of the most painful realizations I've had to deal with is that no man is an island. I grew up as a loner and introvert. I loved my personal space and have almost zero tolerance for intruders. During my first Bachelor's program in Human Anatomy, my class leader aptly tagged me the "one man squad." I got things done faster alone than in a group. In fact, if you wanted to destabilize, render me ineffective, or draw out the worst traits in me, put me in a group. During medical school, student study groups didn't really cut it for me. I worked faster alone and considered group meetings a waste of time. How wrong I was!

The first time I had to work as part of a group in Hopkins, I let my group members and leader know that I sucked at group work. In fact, my synergy with the group was so poor I ended up with a grade of "C" in a vital course. That shook me and I decided to change my perspective and attitude. The next time I worked in a group, we blazed a grade "A" that was almost a 100% in scores! The difference in both groups was the passion we shared in our work and the level of respect we had for each other. Regardless, I had learnt my lesson; two people of like minds can easily get a job done in no time, with mind-blowing results.

"One can chase a thousand and two put ten thousand to flight" (Deuteronomy 32:30a&b)

4. Believe in yourself
I've heard people refer to confidence as sexy and attractive. I've heard people refer to confidence as sexy and attractive. As far as I'm concerned, and I sincerely believe this to be the truth, it is a survival skill.
So you have a new product you're working on and you keep thinking *"I can't do this,"* believe me, you will never be able to succeed at it. A huge aspect of success and overcoming the struggles in your way is, believing you have the ability to

make good things happen. You don't have to feel it, just believe it. Confidence dampens fears and worries, and boosts your morale. A person with high morale does not easily succumb to distractions. He is focused on his trademark, his brand. And no, you don't have to be an entrepreneur or a manager to need or demonstrate this trait; everyone needs it to be a success in the littlest task.

After I broke my leg, I struggled to keep up at school for the ensuing three weeks. At the beginning of the third week, I went into the MPH program office and told my program coordinator, *"I can't do this; for the first time in my life I am uttering the words, I can't do this."* I meant I couldn't cope with school. The distractions were abounding. I was breaking down. Before the accident, I had enrolled for 20 courses for the term but luckily I didn't get approved for a 4-credit course because the class was filled and so I had 16 credits left to cover. But my plate still felt too full, heavily full. And with two kids with virtually no help (I had a baby-sitter who stayed with Kay while I was at school but that was all she did; everything else was my business!), I was faint.

I have always prided myself in being strong, boasted about it even; but for the first time, I saw failure ahead of me and I embraced it. My coordinator looked at me and read out my "requirements" for maintaining legal non-immigrant status, especially the number of onsite credits I had to take to remain in status. Of course he was sympathetic but he didn't make the laws. He called the International office on my behalf and I was asked to get a letter from my doctor highlighting the reason for my difficulty.

I got the letter in a couple of days but never forwarded it. Why? Because, after I left the office, I thought about it and decided to see my left fibular fracture and right ankle sprain for what they were: distractions! I built back my confidence, and while some of my colleagues complained about their course-load for the term, I completed my 16-credits with passing grades. I survived.

Confidence is a survival trait. The moment you lose it, your ship starts sinking. No one is going to believe in you for long if you don't believe in yourself. Even if you're blessed with supportive people who believe in your abilities, you'll still have to build your self-belief. The best that external support can do for you in the face of distractions, is reassure you. The groundwork is yours, all yours!

5. Take a break; don't break the pace

How many times have you heard the words, "walk away?" Many of us were told from childhood, to count to 10 when angry, in a bid to diffuse our emotions and prevent embarking on actions we may regret. The same rule applies to handling distractions. Not in the exact context, but close.

Sometimes, handling distractions requires us to walk away from compromising situations. There is no point attending certain events or staying for drinks when you're an alcoholic in an AA program; avoid the distraction. If you have friends or acquaintances whose associations put you in the path of failure, walk away. If you're trying to keep your family expenditure within budget because you need to save or your income isn't so great at the moment, there's no point window-shopping at the Hermes store or eyeing a pair of Manolo Blahniks in catalogues; walk away.

Not Breaking the Pace

I didn't always know how to handle relationships. As a matter of fact, I only recently started making an effort to make difficult relationships work. I was very good at walking away from hurtful people; which happened to be a lot by the way because I'm a very sensitive person. So this means my circle has always been very small and close-knit. I had the ability to walk away from anyone once they crossed me. Right now I know better. I'm not in any way close to perfection and I realize I hurt people too! So, one of my recent goals has been to make my relationships work, regardless of how many times I am hurt. In the course of this resolution, I discovered something very powerful, "Not breaking the pace."

I didn't know what it was until I consciously did it the first time. I was on the phone with a friend, one with whom I shared some really good business interests and in the course of our conversation, he said something out of line and refused to apologize. In my usual fashion, I was ready to retreat and put a few bars in the relationship. Instead I quickly assessed the situation, remembered my resolve and politely asked to end the call. As soon as I did, I let out some steam and resumed other tasks. Not surprisingly, I was fine and nobody got hurt. I didn't break the friendship, didn't speak in anger and didn't hurt anyone because I was annoyed. I took myself to a spot where I could handle my emotions while still holding all that was dear exactly the way it was. Simply put, I took a break but I didn't break the pace!

This principle is applicable to every goal. When one or many hurdles distract you from your goal, I encourage you to see the light at the end of the tunnel. Remember what treasure accomplishing that goal holds for you. Don't ever lose sight of your desires but take time to exhale and go back to the drawing board. Remember, Steve Jobs couldn't get the public to buy into his NeXT Inc. operating system but within a year, Apple Inc. bought over NeXT Inc. for $429 million and Steve was back at Apple as the boss. It's okay to walk away for a while, but don't lose your vision in the process; don't break your pace. This is what makes true champions, knowing when to fight, and when to stop for refreshment. A dogged soldier is a dead soldier.

Illustration Format: Overcoming Distractions

iFormat 4

Bernard Lewis is an alcoholic. He grew up in a poor, disorganized neighborhood and constantly got in fights. Now at 26, Bernard has a mile-long rap sheet and can't seem to stay out of trouble. Most of his troubles can be traced to his history of alcohol abuse. Bernard first tasted alcohol at twelve and became addicted to it as he aged. In the past two years he's been in and out of several AA programs but has been unable to overcome his addiction.

Bernard has one major problem; that is, the company he keeps. Although his friends aren't all alcoholics, they love to party and hang out around bars. Even though Bernard has repeatedly tried to commit to change, he finds it tough to maintain sobriety for long periods of time. As a result, he's wasting away, unable to accomplish much in his life.

Application

Apparently, Bernard's vision is to stay sober. To reach this, he must quit alcohol use. Unfortunately, he's been unable to achieve this goal. Just like other people with diverse visions, Bernard faces distractions/challenges on the way to achieving his vision.

Analysis/Sample iFormat

1. Identify your vision. The first thing Bernard needs to do is re-identify his vision. Does he still wish to be sober? If he does, he needs to accept this as the ultimate goal. If he wants to pursue sobriety as the final goal or attain it as a means to a greater vision, such as holding down a job or maintaining a relationship, then he needs to focus appropriately. For instance, his thought trend could be, "I need to remain sober so I can hold a job or save my relationship.

2. Identify the overarching distractions to achieving your goal. For Bernard, the two main distractions are attending parties and the company he keeps. He needs to walk away from these compromising situations and surround himself with men of like passion or vision.

3. Create a vivid mental picture of what you want to see accomplished. In Bernard's case he needs to visualize a steady job, or a stable relationship, and place value on these outcomes. He has to hold these mental images and consciously walk towards them. It may not be easy at first but applying the lessons from the first three chapters makes it easier. No matter what you dream, it is achievable if you think it, believe it, determine to reach it and stay focused. In

times of discouragement, overcome fear with faith and speak the word of faith in line with God's word.

4. Remain consistent. Success is not a destination; it is a process. For everyday Bernard stays away from alcohol, a goal is accomplished that will ultimately bring him to the big picture. Basking in these small achievements refreshes the mind to continue pressing towards success.

5. Believe in yourself. Continuously viewing yourself as a failure isn't going to do much to get you closer to success. If anything, it will turn you in the opposite direction. No failure succeeds but success comes to those who wait (work; right attitude, have interest and who stay tough). Be confident that you can achieve whatever it is you set your heart on. Confidence does not entail foolhardiness. Bernard was wrong to attend parties and spend evenings out with his former drink buddies. Confidence is useful when applied with the right ingredients, not when it is mixed with explosives. Rely on yourself (start with God) for strength and not other people. This prevents relapse when others fail you or when you're faced with frustrations.

6. Pray.

CHAPTER FIVE
THE POWER OF PRAYER

The one thing that has been constant in my life is prayer. Sometimes, praying is a way for me to overcome distractions and become refreshed. It is also a way for me to keep confessing my desires to God until they are achieved.

"Delight yourself also in the LORD; and he shall give you the desires of your heart. Commit your way unto the LORD; trust also in him; and he shall bring it to pass." (Psalm 37:4&5)

Even though I accepted Christ into my life as a teenager, I wasn't always fervent or faithful. One amazing thing I have found though, is that God does love me specially and I know He feels that same way about you too. The Bible does state, *"He's no respecter of persons."* (Acts 10:34). I wholly recognize, accept, and profess that I am nothing without Him. Everything I have achieved in life came at a price, one that He always provided. And I'm not saying it for completeness sake. Without God, I wouldn't have made it this far, wouldn't have survived even.

A while ago, I started a health blog, which was hosted on Google. I wanted to invest some money on publicity to generate traffic but my resources always needed to be diverted elsewhere. Even though I didn't make it appear that way, the blog was actually business for me. I saw it as part of my office and when it did not generate income, I began to lose interest. Now, everyone who does online business or marketing understands the need for traffic. I needed hits and better conversion rates than I was getting from Google+ or Facebook. Unfortunately, there was "zero budget" to accomplish this. I resorted to prayer.

During monthly or weekly services at Church, I consistently prayed for traffic. It took a while but one day, I saw the Facebook page I had created for the blog receive "likes" from people I knew weren't on my friend's list; complete strangers! Initially I was shocked, and I scanned through my settings to see if I had accidentally set up a Facebook Ad. Nothing! Then, I remembered. Whoohoo! God answers prayers. Every time I put up a blog post after then, I got much better hit rates and the traffic I needed began to build and come my way. As I write this, the "likes" are still coming through.

I mentioned earlier that I repeatedly asked God for three specific things when I was pregnant. I'll share them here. Truth is, when I lifted up my desires in prayer, I was always aware I was not qualified to be in God's good books but I prayed anyway. The more I think of it, the more I realize that prayers and the answers I received kept me through my moments of darkness. I have battled pain, heartbreak, disease, extreme circumstances, poverty and shame. I have had frustration stare me in the face. Everything I touched failed. Many times, I called myself a failure. When people hailed and admired me in public, I had demons to fight behind closed doors. I have fought hard, struggled to points where I completely gave up and wanted to die. Yes, at some point I did want to die.

One night, during my NYSC days, I picked up a breadknife in the kitchen and was contemplating ending it all. Luckily, my friend woke up from sleep and walked in the kitchen. I don't know what would have happened if nobody had come in. It was all blurry for me then. I was battling an intensely unstable relationship and under pressure from my family. I was simply battered.

Some years later, I understood how people who committed suicide might have felt just before they ended their lives. I don't think they feel pain or any emotion. Emotions keep you alive; they keep you in the flesh. I felt intensely empty. It didn't matter how many accolades I had gathered or how many people tagged me their inspiration; I sunk deep in despair. I knew I needed help but I called on no one. God kept me. The next morning I was calm, and collected. I knew I had descended the pits of hell and God had brought me out. Today, I can boldly say, I am a champion! Not because I am as strong and determined as others think, but because He shows me mercy. If there's anything I can tell you for sure, it's that He answers. He answers anyone who calls. But you must first believe in Him. Today, I stand firm and strong in Him.

"For the scripture saith, whosoever believeth on him shall not be ashamed." (Romans 10:11)

Let me share a short true story. Sometime in 2011, I went to bed with a lit candle placed on top a chest of plastic drawers. I hadn't meant to sleep off but I was tired after a long day at work and chores. The electricity had gone out but I needed to pack my daughter's school and lunch bags for the next day.

So, with my clothes still on, I got in bed to tuck her in but dozed off. When I woke up, the chest was on fire. I don't mean some small gentle flames; it was real hot, smoky fire. I was scared beyond description and I screamed "Jesus" many times. As I screamed, He showed up. I remember where He stood and how He looked but it wasn't a physical image. I can only tell you His eyes were deeply loving and utterly piercing. I'll stop there.

Even though I had screamed so hard, none of my neighbors heard. There were several generators running and the noise was enough to drown out my screams. Thankfully, I got my daughter out of the room and put out the fire. The amazing thing is, my Bible was on the chest of drawers; but the fire did not singe a pinch of it. The flames circled and curved around where the Bible lay but ceased to burn within a hair's breadth of it. The Bible was completely intact and I still use it till date. This may seem like an insignificant story but I cannot miss the power I experienced that night. It's the power of the One to whom I, we, pray.

During my first pregnancy, I thought about some things I really wanted to see happen. I prayed about them constantly every time I went on my knees, morning and night. These are the three things I have severally referred to. This was my first time going to the delivery room but there were certain experiences I didn't want to have. I ceaselessly prayed against receiving an episiotomy or any other cut for that matter, caesarian section inclusive. It may seem unimportant but I was going to have my baby at the beginning of my final year of medical school. I didn't have the time to stay in bed, recovering from a caesarian section or the patience to deal with an episiotomy. So every time I went on my knees, my prayer went thus, " *Dear Lord, I am not going to have any tears or cuts. No caesarian, no episiotomies. Nothing!*" The other two requests were for my daughter. I wanted her pretty and smart. God answered.

These prayer requests were the first through which I encountered the power of the prayer of faith. You may wonder what I mean. You may even ask, didn't God answer your prayers before then? Yes He did; very many times. Nonetheless, there were times I asked for things that I deemed important but didn't get them. I was fixed on asking once in faith, but it didn't always come through; and I don't know why not but I despaired. Some people say, when you ask something from God, just do it once. They explain that this is the demonstration of faith and that repetition constitutes faithlessness. I believed them. It may be true for them. But it didn't always work for me and I'll share what did.

Every time I repeatedly prayed about a need or desire, it was easier for me to exercise faith; it worked and I always received that which I asked. So I have stuck to this plan. If I want something, I'm asking God for it every time in prayer and believing through faith that I have received. It works, every time! Try it.

On the day I went in to the delivery room, I wasn't even in labor. Labor was induced and I progressed rapidly. Within four hours I was in the worst pain imaginable. An induced labor without anesthesia is possibly the most painful experience a woman can have. In the midst of my pain, I no longer cared if I was cut or not. I just wanted it over with and if cutting me in a million places would get me there, I thought, so be it. But I didn't say a word to *the Obs and Gynae* senior resident who came in to take the delivery. I never told him I didn't want an episiotomy nor did I express my change of heart. However, as I got in the delivery suite, I heard him tell the midwife, *"I'm not going to cut her."* I knew instantly, that Someone had gone ahead of me to prepare a miracle because this was a center where, typically, every woman having a baby for the first time got the nick. My baby's birth weight was 3.75kg and we got through it with perineal massage. Anybody else could have taken the delivery on that day, but God had His instrument waiting in the wings!

The second time round, I made the same request to Him, like a mantra. Even though my little lady weighed 3.76kg, we got by without an episiotomy. And no, I am not that endowed. It was a simple prayer of faith. My sisters asked me how I did it; I told them to, *"pray."* I trust God with the most serious and silliest of things. That is the easiest summary of my success thus far. I keep praying because it's cheaper than running water. And it works. His blessings are free; all I have to do is ask! Repeatedly!

"And he spake a parable unto them to this end, that men ought always to pray, and not to faint; Saying, There was in a city a judge, which feared not God, neither regarded man: And there was a widow in that city; and she came unto him, saying, Avenge me of mine adversary. And he would not for a while: but afterward he said within himself, Though I fear not God, nor regard man; Yet because this widow troubleth me, I will avenge her, lest by her continual coming she weary me. And the

Lord said, hear what the unjust judge saith. And shall not God avenge his own elect, which cry day and night unto him, though he bear long with them?" (Luke 18:1-7)

If the unjust judge gave in to the widow's repeated demands, how much more the One, Who gave up His Son? *Will He not also, with Him, freely give us all things*? (Romans 8:32)

As a student in Medical school, I was extremely afraid of the professional exams. Yes I worked hard; I even heard I was very smart. But the fear of the MBBS professional exams got you on your toes and your feet in cold water. I never wanted to sit for an exam twice. Medical students in Nigeria take four professional examinations at the end of the third, fourth fifth and sixth (final) years. We were allowed up to three attempts to pass each of these exams. The first attempt occurs about two weeks after the end of each session; the second attempt typically happens three months after the first attempt and is termed a "re-sit." If a student failed any of the courses during the second attempt, he/she would have to repeat that session to qualify for the third and final attempt a year after.

I wasn't ready to try a second attempt at any level. The third attempt was never in consideration. I was desperate to succeed. What I did was simple, practical and scriptural. I went into a covenant with God, and I said, *"Lord see, I won't cheat or do anything wrong in your sight during my tests and exams; I'll do all that is right and true. I'll study hard, do my part and obey You; and in return, please give me good success."*

There were many tempting events all through school but I can tell you I never fell. There were times some of my classmates, who were also my neighbors, attempted purported exam questions hours before the exams commenced. I was never moved. In fact, people dreaded to come to me with such criminal practices. In my fourth year, a close friend who was ahead of me in Med school, called me up and asked me to *"go to the flat upstairs and look through the supposedly leaked questions."* I told her I had no such desire. Her response was, *"when the time comes, I'll laugh at you."* She implied I would fail the exams and then she would laugh at me for having been stubborn and missing an opportunity. Instantly, she gave me a prayer hold; *"dear Lord, she will laugh with me and not at me."*

I have no idea how my neighbors got access to the exam questions but the irony was every one of them failed the exams. Some of them repeated the year! Till date, I pray before taking any examination. It doesn't matter how much time I have or how well I prepared, I take time to pray because I know, *"It is not of him that willeth, nor of him that runneth, but of God that sheweth mercy."* (Romans 9:16)

And oh yes, my friend laughed with me! All through medical school, I never had to sit for an exam twice. Even when I had a difficult pregnancy and dealt with intense emotional heartache, the mercies of God kept me. I did my part, but it was God Who finished it and ensured that my best was good enough. He answered me every time I prayed.

Believing God Through Impossibilities

My life has been marked by so many miracles that at one point, my husband called me, *"a miracle on two legs."* It was so apt.

Two physicians at the college hospital where I had my internship training separately told me I looked like someone who had a connective tissue disorder. I rejected it deep down in my heart and was angry within my spirit.

A couple of years later, I received a diagnosis of "Cholelithiasis" (Gall bladder disease/ stone) from one of these physicians. It wasn't just a shot in the dark. I had the symptoms, signs and even some risk factors down to the letter! I was scared and I turned to my husband, then partner, for sympathy, he gave me none. That was the best thing he did for me. For if he had sympathized with me, I would have accepted the diagnosis and that would have been a fatal mistake. He pointed me to God; he always does that, and I love him deeply for it.

The Physician whose patient I had become, ordered several investigations, including a connective tissue screening for anti-DNA antibodies that was sent to South Africa for analysis. One night, after a failed attempt to elicit sympathy from my husband, I took a chair and went to sit out under the stars. I do not remember the precise words I said in prayer but I poured out my heart to my Creator. I bared my soul, knowing He is the only way out.

A couple of days later, every test result, including radiological investigations, came back negative. I haven't had a symptom since then. God heard my prayers. He healed and fixed every thing that was wrong.

A few weeks before I received my admission letter to study for my MPH at Hopkins, I discovered I was pregnant. I was ready to have a second baby but I was still unmarried and living with my partner of eight years. This isn't a situation I recommend or advocate for anyone; it was my personal circumstance, most of it decided and allowed by me but fraught with real life issues, nonetheless. All through that time, I struggled with my spirituality.

Frankly, many situations in life will cause us spiritual struggles. Mine was mine.

Within a few weeks of the pregnancy test turning out positive, I began experiencing severe left sided lumbar pains; I spotted a little but the cramps were what kept me writhing in pain at night. An ultrasound scan at one of the most popular and recommended centers in the city revealed an ectopic pregnancy. I cannot even begin to describe how I felt. The one thing I have never wanted to experience is surgery. And surgery for an ectopic pregnancy was even worse. I imagined the procedure, the recovery time; worst of all, I thought of the complications of the surgery. It wasn't a pleasant thought train.

In my worried state, I called a professor of "Obs and Gynae," who had been my teacher and with whom I had worked as an intern, and narrated my story. He asked me to go to his clinic and repeat an abdomino-pelvic scan in preparation for an explorative laparotomy. Surgery! With every passing moment, the procedure seemed more likely, and the reality of the situation sunk deeper. I had almost lost a sister to a similar condition; I wasn't ready to go through it too. I thought, why me? Why now?

As I moved to go the hospital, my partner called me up on the phone and said, *"let's go to Church and see Papa."* By Papa, he meant the President and founder of Salvation Ministries worldwide, Pastor David Ibiyeomie. I was hesitant. I wasn't even a member of the Church then. I am a doctor and well aware of the dangers and indices associated with delays in ectopic pregnancy cases. I didn't know how bad this case was and I didn't want to progress to a ruptured ectopic in a place where I could not readily access medical help. My partner (husband) had thought better.

God is always the Only way out. I eventually conceded; after all, it wouldn't hurt to pray before going into the theatre.

When we got to the Church, impatience was written all over me. I was agitated. My mind whirred with the technicalities of everything that was possibly happening on my insides.

It wasn't long before we found out pastor David wasn't in the office. My heart shook with fear; oh how I needed him to pray for me just then! His absence set me off even worse. Finally, three pastors prayed and lifted up my request before God. One had asked me what I desired, and I told him *"I wanted to be married and have my baby safely."* I didn't bother pretending we were married. I needed a miracle and I wasn't taking any chances. My partner was asked the same question and his response was same as mine.

After the prayers, I stepped into the bathroom to anoint my abdomen and instantly, I felt something pop. On the way back from the hospital, another Pastor, the founder of Pacesetters Assembly, called in and prayed for me. The follow up scan showed a pregnancy in utero (within my womb).

Less than four months later, I married the love of my life in a beautiful ceremony. Months later, I had my amazing little daughter. Do you still doubt that God answers prayers?

Let me be your testimony.

Illustration Format: Cultivating a prayerful Life

iFormat 5

1. Think of two important things you prayed for and received in the past. Write them down.

2. Try to recall how often you prayed for these requests before you received answers. You may not remember the exact number of times so you may write once or repeatedly beside each request listed in (1) above.

3. Think of two important requests you prayed about but did not receive. Write them down.

4. Recall how often you prayed for these requests and mark once or repeatedly beside each.

5. Compare your lists. What do you think? Does your faith come alive more when you ask repeatedly or when you ask once?

6. Keep practicing the response to (5) and believe in your heart that you have received (Matthew 21:22).

7. List two important requests associated with your goals/vision. If you already have a list written from the preceding chapters, you're free to use it.

8. Keep your thoughts positive and confess the word of faith as it concerns these goals. Remember to apply the Word (from the Bible) as it concerns your vision/goals/requests.

9. Submit these requests to God every time you pray. Always give thanks.

CHAPTER SIX
WINNERS DON'T BOW TO SHAME OR PAIN

"For your shame, I'll give you double." (Isaiah 61:7)

In the past year I have been confronted with more shameful situations than I have had to deal with my entire life. I have been humbled and severally embarrassed. I know many people who couldn't have handled some of the things I faced. I didn't have a choice. In spite of the situation, I had to hold my head high. As a defense measure, I withdrew deeper into an artificial shell that necessity brought to light. I gave up participation in social gatherings and focused only on the things that mattered. This was my survival strategy. It may not have been the best but it worked.

I had arrived the U.S for school knowing that I was on a tight budget but I had no idea that in the ensuing months, I would have absolutely zero budget. I lived in a hotel for two months before I could move into an apartment. The cost of living in the hotel was far more than the rent for an apartment but I didn't get enough money to settle my bills at the hotel so I could check out and move into an apartment. Initially, I got some good amount of money but the funds usually came in when I had stayed a while and needed to pay bills. Automatically, everything that entered my account was put on hold to pay the hotel.

I was in the hotel when my second daughter was born. After birth, she didn't come home for eight days but eventually she was discharged and we all stayed in the suite together. We hadn't planned to stay in a hotel for long but we didn't have much choice. I didn't have enough to make a rental deposit for an apartment. It was cheaper in the interim to remain at the hotel but in the long term, the cost was more than triple that for renting an apartment.

Eventually, I moved out of the hotel to share a three-bedroom townhouse with another lady who lived with her mom and two kids. Let's just say it wasn't a brilliant arrangement but it sufficed. Thelma (not her real name) was a nice Christian lady. She let me move in on the promise of paying the rent within a few days. At that time, I had a check for $4,000, which I had requested from my partial scholarship to apply towards upkeep but it was yet to clear at the bank. I took up a room on the top floor of the house and settled in as much as I could with my kids. I sincerely looked forward to getting my own place but in the mean time we had a roof over our heads.

When I moved in with Thelma, my intention was to stay for two weeks and then move to a place of my own. I had the check from school and I hoped and believed we could handle our own place. As I hunted for an affordable apartment in a good neighborhood, I often had to go back and forth with the same agents. It was during one of such contemplations that I got hurt.

It was precisely the day after the end of my first term at Hopkins. I had stayed at Thelma's place for a month, two weeks longer than we had intended and I was unsettled. Even though we had paid the month's rent, I wasn't at ease because the new school year was about to begin and I needed to find a school for my daughter. The only way to do that was to get an apartment in a decent area and get her registered in the zone school. That fateful Saturday felt like the perfect day to finalize house-hunting plans and begin my move. Even though I had initially vowed not to leave the house on that day because my legs ached from having walked a long distance the previous day, I prepared to go out anyway. I had a 2pm appointment with an agent and I wanted to keep it.

As I went down the stairs, with my baby nestled on my right shoulder and a car seat in my left hand, I slipped on a step, twisted both ankles awkwardly and tumbled down. My baby who was 12weeks old at the time flew out of my arms and hit the floor before I did. I lay on the floor screaming because I couldn't go to her. I was in severe pain and couldn't even crawl. Thelma heard me and ran down the stairs, picked my baby up and assured me she was okay. I didn't believe her and I kept on screaming.

Those moments on the floor were the scariest of my life. I had no thought for myself, or the pain I felt. Fear for my 12week-old baby engulfed me. I had no idea how she'd landed. I didn't know if anything was broken and I couldn't bear it. In about half an hour we were transported to the Johns Hopkins hospital in an ambulance. I was more than relieved when she got a clean bill of health at the ER. My case was a different story. After five hours in the hospital, I got the verdict: I had fractured my left fibula and sustained severe right ankle sprain. I took the news with all the courage I could muster. I saw my two-week holiday, which I had looked forward to, disappear before my eyes but that was the least of my worries. Other projects came to an abrupt halt. All of a sudden, moving out to my own place ceased to be an emergency. I had to focus on being back on my feet. It wasn't as easy as I thought. Or wished.

I was discharged from the emergency room with casts on both legs and orders not to put any weight on my left leg. Although the sprain caused my right leg to be substantially more painful, it was the only leg with which I could walk. Before I left the ER, the doctor from the orthopedic unit assured me that the cast over the fracture would be replaced with an air cast after two weeks and I would be allowed to put some weight on the fractured leg. Two weeks later, the cast was changed but I wasn't allowed to put any weight on the leg and I had to keep using crutches. I think I took a couple of painkillers within the first 24 hours but I doubt I completed a 48-hour dose. Most analgesics are secreted into the breast milk and because I was a nursing mother, I refrained.

When I got back to Thelma's apartment that night, I couldn't get out of the cab. With each body movement, no matter how little, came searing pains. The pain was much worse on the sprained foot. But that was the only foot on which I was allowed to bear weight. I battled to get out of the cab but I couldn't make it in the house. Some neighbors came to help support me, propping me up on either side but my right leg would not budge. It refused to obey any motion signals from my brain. The pain was eleven over ten! I gave up, got on all fours and crawled into the house. I made it into the living room but still had two flights of stairs to go before getting to my room.

I had declined a move by Thelma to move my mattress down to the living room. How long would I stay in the living room, I thought. There was no bathroom on the ground floor and more than anything else, I needed my privacy that night. I needed my time to cry alone. My life had just drastically changed. I had no idea how I was going to care for two kids, one of whom was just an infant, in my state.

I finally made it up the stairs and got in bed. It was no mean feat but I gave it everything. In those moments, even while in severe pain, my heart was intensely glad. My daughter was fine. She had hit the floor and could have sustained severe injuries but there wasn't a scratch on her. When she flew out of my arms, I repeatedly called on God, screaming "Jesus, Jesus," countless times before calling out for Thelma. As I later told my sister, I sincerely believe He showed up, caught Kay and dropped her gently on the floor.

There was no other explanation. My sister had whined an *"I wish He caught you too;"* I didn't know it then, and I was content that my baby was fine.

Eventually, I realized He caught me too. If He hadn't, let's just say a fibular fracture and sprain would have seemed like a plate of pancakes with eggs. I was grateful; I still am.

As the days passed, the expression on my older daughter's face completely broke my heart. She couldn't bear to see me crawl. Every time I crawled up or down the stairs, her eyes filled with tears and she would turn away. It was painful to behold. My heart broke beyond measure; the wrench in my guts was raw and deep. It took some time before I realized that she thought I would never walk again. I tried to reassure her that with time we would dance around the house but I don't think she believed me. She was only six and had to watch our lives change so immensely. My heart wept for the situation she was caught in.

The morning after I was let out of the ER was probably the toughest for me. I woke up early and needed to use the bathroom. I tried to crawl out of bed into bathroom, which was en-suite. I made it as far as the floor beside the mattress. And even that took more effort than I could muster. I woke up my six-year old daughter and asked her to get me a bucket from the bathroom. She did, calmly and dutifully. This wonderful child of mine became my nurse and for two weeks she took good care of me. I do not exaggerate when I say I don't think anyone else could have been as patient, loving and caring as she was. She hated to see me down but she made sure she helped in any way she could. I never knew, heard of, or saw a more responsible six-year old.

Within the week, my doctor wrote the U.S embassy in my home country, asking that my mother be granted a travel visa so she could come care for the kids and I. It was honored but she couldn't make it for another one month. My little nurse was all I had.

The stairs in Thelma's apartment were partly responsible for my fall. On my first day in the house, Thelma's first warning had been *"be careful on the stairs, there's something not quite right with them."* The carpet on the stairs was old and worn. It didn't make for a good grip under the feet. As a matter of fact, the carpet was slippery and we all had to be wary. The stair below the one on which I slipped had an acute and narrow curve that made it impossible for it to support both my feet when I landed. Instead my ankles contorted so horribly that my bone broke before I hit the floor. I know because I heard the sound.

A few days after the accident, I crawled down the stairs to the kitchen for the first time. I had to cook so my daughter would have something decent to eat. She had lived on bread and biscuits for two days and it was time to feed her something more nourishing. I made it through on one leg; or almost. Just as I finished cooking, I slid and fell. I stayed on the floor helpless and near hopeless. I needed a shoulder and some comfort. Thelma came to help me up but she was none too pleased I had attempted cooking by myself, in my state. She was upset because I didn't let her do the cooking. How could I have? I had little left to hold on to. Being able to care for my children was one. I fell many more times after that but I got myself up.

The good part of having food stored up in the refrigerator was that I didn't have to go down the stairs every time we needed to eat. Whenever Thelma was home, I'd ask her to help warm some food in the microwave and then my daughter would bring the plates up the stairs to our room. The meals weren't regular because Thelma often went to the library to study but we got by. My daughter made us tea severally and served it with bread or biscuits; depending on her preference, she was the boss! She helped bring clean water into the room for her sister's bath and tossed the bath water after I emptied the baby tub into a bucket. This went on for a while. Gradually, I was able to crawl into the bathroom by myself even though getting up or going back on all fours was challenging. If I'd had a choice, I would have preferred to fight Floyd than go through with the pain. But I had to live with my fate. I was determined to put the past behind me as soon as I could and vowed within me that I would wear heels during my graduation (which was eight months away).

About two weeks after the fall, I stood for the first time. This was when I knew for sure that my older daughter really thought I'd never walk again; and she did not believe me when I told her I still would. When she saw me stand, she screamed loudly with surprise. I didn't stay on my "foot" for too long but for as long as I did, shrieks of *"she can stand, she can stand,"* rent the air. I was moved by her joy.

When the next school term resumed, I insisted on getting back to lectures and the orthopedic unit provided me with a knee walker. That way, I could flex the fractured leg on the walker, which looked like a mini tricycle, and ride with my right foot on the ground, to the bus stop and catch the bus to school. It was like hopping very fast but the walker hardly provided a smooth ride. The tires were rigid and tubeless, and as I rode/moved, they were easily destabilized by the bumps on the sidewalk. As there were many bumps, the chances of losing balance and tipping over was almost a ten. Thankfully, both of my legs were firmly held in casts so I didn't sustain more injuries. I never knew how useful the cast over my sprained ankle was until I tried walking without it. Let me just say I learnt my lesson and made sure I had both casts in place at all times.

A few weeks after the accident, I moved out of Thelma's place. Although I could now stand, I still wasn't allowed to put any weight on the fractured leg. Kay's nanny made our move easy. She showed up with her mom and moved all our stuff into waiting cabs. She also helped me shop for groceries and did her utmost to get us settled in. She was an angel.

Moving into my own place seemed like the best thing that happened to us. I hadn't really settled in since I arrived and finally I could lie down without fear or worry. It was good for two months. I was already at my own place when I received the knee walker and resumed school again. It wasn't easy wheeling myself to the bus stop with my daughter in tow so I could get her to school, and then ride another eight blocks to catch my bus to Hopkins. This happened for a few weeks and in that time I fell off the walker several times but thankfully without any additional injuries.

There was the one time I fully went over the knee walker before hitting the ground as I fell. I was on my way to pick my daughter after school and was late. Her school office frowned aggressively at late "pick-up" and I wasn't in the mood for a lecture from the administrators. I tried to move as fast as one leg and a knee walker would allow but fate wasn't a willing accomplice. The tires of the walker hit a bump; I lost my balance and suffered a nasty fall. I got up but mentally psyched myself to slow down.

As I went through all of this, I was no longer much to look at as a woman. I was a dark shadow of my old self. My hair was near unkempt and I didn't have any decent clothes. My clothes were so worn, it didn't matter how often I washed them; they looked dirty still. No one who knew me would have recognized me. My skin color was at least, six shades darker than my original complexion. I never thought of wearing any make-up. What was the point? There was no motivation. My hair was cut short and undone. No one could relate the "me" I had become with my picture that adorned the Hopkins site as a student ambassador. There was nothing physically attractive about my appearance. But I struggled on. I felt shamed and inadequate deep down but I had learnt to hold my head high against all odds. And this I did.

I know many people felt sorry for me and could tell just by looking at me that I was going through really rough times. I could tell the pity on their faces. I learned not to care. I had come here to better my education and get trained at the world's best school of public health. I was determined to get that education. I forged on.

As the months ran by, my rent deposit ran out. I had believed my husband when he gave me positive reassurance about his business coming together but somehow everything seemed to fall apart at the last minute. It was like a poet once said, *"things fall apart, the center cannot hold."*
I can't forget how firmly my mom stood by me. When she arrived a month after I broke my leg, she was shocked to see me. I saw her shed tears. But I didn't know she wept for more than my scarred legs. She wept for the "me" she saw.

My mom had always seen me as the "flashy" one among her kids. I always did stuff that made me stand out. It didn't have to be expensive; I just always put my stamp on it. I would redesign my clothes after they came in from the tailors. My "aso-ebi" attire at any wedding was always different. I either redid my outfit or I touched it up. I loved to dress up. Like many females, I always had a weave sewn in and even though I am blessed with good hair, hardly anyone saw it. The weaves came off in the salon and were put back in within a few hours. I remember being nicknamed the "glamor girl with a difference" by my colleagues at school. I cared about how I looked even though I was more serious about my academics.

I wasn't particularly born into a rich home. We were just about average but with time, I learnt the necessities to make myself presentable. My husband also spoilt me as much as he could. He was always generous but life changed.

I could understand my mom's shock when she saw me. I had on clothes that people in homeless shelters would have tossed. Even deep in the winter, I could neither afford a winter jacket nor gloves. Indeed, I went through an entire winter without a pair of gloves. Maryland isn't the friendliest of places during the winter but the $5 for gloves was rather put towards food. Money was that tight.

When momsie (that's what we call her) came, she took over most of the bills. I know her business suffered because she spent so much. She told one of my siblings, *"I've never seen your sister look this way, but I admire her courage to push through in spite of all."* My dad never ceased to tell me how proud he was that I held my head up despite it all. My parents were an amazing rock. Had my mom not shown up when she did, I might have broken down. Her presence helped me handle a lot of issues. I was able to stay back at school after lectures to finish up assignments and tests. I had a lot of backlog and understandably so. A couple of faculty members were sympathetic, understanding why I missed a few days of school but others wanted assignments and tests turned in by the deadlines. It was not uncommon to see a lone woman hopping on one foot with the other propped on a knee walker, rolling down the bus path near Hopkins, just before 8pm every night that October.

It all paid off. Without dropping any of my course loads, I finished the term, on one leg and in good academic standing. Hopkins is not an easy school. The work is tasking. Some of my classmates always complained and I laughed at them. Most were single, with no immediate family, and I often told them, *"If you complain, what should I do?"* One actually tried to convince me her situation was worse than mine because she had two nephews at home that she had to care for. I was very amused but I didn't let it show. She lived with her aunt and her two kids. She definitely had no idea! I smiled and ended the conversation.

Without God's mercies and my family support, I wouldn't have made it through.

I was still a hopper on one foot when my mom's six-week leave from work expired and she had to get back to work. I understood that. She had done a lot in the six weeks she'd spent with us and for that alone I was inspired to keep fighting. I ignored shame and told her what happened with my husband's business. The losses he suffered were not restricted to him alone. It was a loss in hundreds of millions spread across several investors and their families. There is a ton of drama surrounding this story that I would perhaps one day share in another book.

My mom never knew we had lost so much and when I told her, she was shocked. She didn't understand how I kept strong through it all. Truth is, I wasn't and I'm still not that very strong. My first name literally translates to "soft." I am sensitive and touchy; I cry over the littlest things. There is only one craze I have; one craze I cultivated; that is the intense desire to succeed; the fierce need to make an impact on my generation. I am never content with mediocrity. I learnt early that being poor did not translate to being mediocre. If it did, there would be no Apple Inc. today; there would be no Ben Carson, neurosurgeon extraordinaire. All over the world, many men and women have defied great odds to change the tides of their time. They were my mentors.

Look at Hillary Clinton. There is only one word to describe her. Inspirational! Many women would have crumbled over the high profile scandal her family suffered. Her pain, misery, and the shame she must have felt could have shut her down. She could have succumbed to the media pressure and hid her face and the rest of her family away from the public eye forever. But not Hilary! She's still kicking and doing really good. She embraced her pain and made the most out of it. She stood her ground and continued with her dreams. She did not let circumstance deter or intimidate her. She has entered masculine territories and excels. Hilary does not fear the glass ceiling. Like Ben Carson, Senator Clinton may well be on her way to becoming America's next President. Even if neither succeeds, it wouldn't matter; they already are legends.

After I had my first baby, my cousin called me aside and said to me; *"How did you do it? The shame would have killed me. How did you keep at school being a pregnant unwed mother?"* I simply laughed at her. This was someone who was more worldly-wise than I was, confessing that she couldn't handle shame. It seemed funny. But the truth is, just like I did at Hopkins, I blocked out shame. It would have been a distraction otherwise. My eyes were focused on some other prize. Shame wasn't going to help me get it. So, I fixed my eyes on the prize. Not once did my head come down in public. I had a wonderful friend, who stood by me, unwavering through it all. It never mattered what people said behind me. She never told it to me and it never showed. She is the definition of the word friend. So, I kept shame at bay; I reached for the prize. I got it. I lost nothing.

The week after my mom travelled back to Nigeria, Kay's nanny returned. She wasn't happy I reduced her pay (I had to) but I had also cut down on her number of workdays too.

My budget was slim. I was happy to have a familiar face take over from my mom and watch my baby while I began a new term at school. Kay's nanny never quite understood that paying her weekly was a sacrifice. It was reward for her labor nonetheless and duly deserved but it was by no means affordable. It was a necessity that was made compulsory by my need to be at school. I remember almost having a meltdown when I didn't have the $300 to pay her one weekend. It wasn't a beautiful experience or sight. Thankfully, I was rescued.

At this point, I had no choice but to keep pressing. If I stopped, then I'd have to leave the country. That didn't seem like a bad idea but I couldn't handle all the ramifications and requirements. I didn't have the fare home for three persons. I was yet to pick up Kay's birth certificate, not to mention her travel passport. If I tried to solve the issues by declaring an intention to leave, I'd have only 15days to remain a legal non-immigrant within the country. The birth certificate cost only $28 but even that amount was a huge deal. There were weeks I went by without seeing or spending that amount of money. I simply couldn't afford it. The thought of getting us all ready to leave within two weeks was scary and impractical. I had no choice. I kept pressing.

At some point I regretted not having applied early for some extra scholarship that could have made our lives easier. We had thought we could handle it. The months leading up to my arrival in the U.S had been very promising and we felt the extra cost was well within our means. My hubby had made several investments that were meant to pay out handsomely. But everything had crumbled quicker than a pack of cards.

I didn't want to dwell on the regret for too long and so I started making moves to apply for scholarships. It was late but I was determined to find something. I called up a couple of old friends and asked for contacts and information. I got a few leads and followed up on them. One of my friends told me about individuals and companies who gave scholarships that weren't publicized and he asked me to spread a wider net. I did. I sent messages to a couple of acquaintances, most of who were highly placed. I asked that would be sponsors contact the school and not send a dime to me. I didn't want anyone to think I was a scam.

A few leads seemed good; the other contacts turned up their noses and never spoke to me again. The message was clear, *"Who send you?"* My answer was simple. *"Nobody."* But this was my fight, my dream. Never mind that it was turning out so tough, I was determined to win. Shame did not know my name; I forgot how the word was spelt or what it meant. At that point, shame meant failure. I wasn't having it.

I was desperate. I sent tons of letters to individuals and organizations. I even wrote to Oprah and the President of my country. I wrote to his special assistants and contacted persons through whom I was sure of access. It was a "no show."

There were times I tried so hard that for effort alone, money should have rained from the sky. I considered working part-time but everything I made would have gone to the nanny. This meant time away from my kids with no money to show for it. As it were, I didn't have enough time to split around studying, lectures and the kids. Besides, the pay wouldn't have helped towards completing my tuition. The jobs weren't waiting exactly out there and the hours I was allowed to work were too few to be meaningful. I needed a miracle, and I needed one fast. Many times, while in the reading room at school, I would begin to weep uncontrollably. The pressure was so intense and I couldn't always handle it. Yet I couldn't let the tears last for too long. There were assignments, tests, and term papers to be turned in. There were exams to be written and passed. As quickly as I cried, I went back to work.

Once I prayed so hard about a breakthrough and I could hear God gently tell me, *"the miracle is in the house."*

I thought about this and refrained from making further contacts for a while. *"The miracle is in the house? Through whom? How? When? Where?"* I didn't get the answers to these questions. I wasn't really sure whom, from within my house or among those close to me, would become my miracle. After a while, I went back to sourcing scholarships or finding a cosigner to float a student loan. Nothing worked. People made promises and turned their backs at the last minute. There were times I pondered on the spirituality of my situation. *"Why would someone raise my hopes so high and then dash them at the crucial minute?"* It didn't make any sense. I became apprehensive, thinking, *"maybe something scares them away."* It happened one too many times. I guess I was determined enough to go on because neither the tears and pain nor the hunger and despair stopped me.

Before I knew it, it was the end of the year. Graduation was now five months away and unknown to me, the toughest months were still ahead. As the New Year approached, the fear for my fate increased. *"How would I make it? How would I do it?"* The end seemed too close to think of walking away to begin all over. There were no losses to cut or gains to save.

There was only one way out. Make it! I am not a quitter and so I'm not really sure what other options were open to me.

I wasn't a die-hard fan of any foreign land either.
I love my country to bits. I always made it clear that I would head back home at the end of my studies. I see Nigeria as virgin ground for public health. I had developed a passion for public health and was very clear on what my dreams, passion and vision were. I wanted to be qualified to defend them before any man. I admit I don't like school (sshhh! None of my friends or family will believe it; but it's truth) but I loved to know things. School was a path I had to tread to get to my treasure.

Well, the year ended pretty fast and I drew up energy for one last fight. I needed to pay almost thirty thousand USD to cover the rest of my tuition. I was determined to get it. I felt guilty asking for help from anyone but I consoled myself with the thought that getting a scholarship didn't mean I was lazy or beggarly. At this point, buying food or paying basic bills was a nightmare. There were times I used the "word of faith" on my baby's food pack to stop it from running out. Whenever I noticed she was almost out of food, I would speak to the pack saying, *"you will not go empty until there is money for a refill."* It always worked.

In spite of the hardship, I felt, if I could get tuition coverage, everything else would fall in place. I depended on the "in-house" (family) for upkeep. One of my friends had asked me to let her know if I ever needed groceries or any food in the house. I promised I would. She is a very smart, young and pretty doctor from Ecuador and I liked her a lot. She was my very first friend at Hopkins and truly nice. But I knew I would never ask. There were days I got by on only water but I never asked. It wasn't pride; I just didn't think it was right.

Just before the end of the year, I got in touch with two very good media persons and asked for help in finding individual or corporate scholarship. I asked that they verify my status at school and not have to directly deal with me because of the fear of fraudsters. One of them got back to me with positive news. She promised she knew several persons who could provide the scholarship without blinking. I was in the ninth cloud. Finally; finally I could exhale. I took a deep breath, and held it because just before I could let it out she returned with some bad news. She was no longer excited, because according to her, people only helped when it was a matter of life or death. I let out the air, slowly. I chose to keep faith. It wasn't long before she came back with more news for me. I read her email with a stony heart. Her contacts asked her to tell me to pack my stuff and go home. They were willing to pay my fare, or at least that was how I understood it. Once, I may have jumped on the offer but not this time. My spirits sunk but I allowed the moment to pass.

Shame is an emotion that allows others to gain control of us. Shame is accepting derogation for situations over which you may or may not have any control. Shame is what you feel when you fear that others will compare your actions or situation with "their" standards and you will fall short. It makes you feel inadequate and worthless. It is okay to feel shame sometimes but it is totally wrong to dwell in it. Shame is humiliation and it can break the strongest of men. Just like pain, shame is a thing of the mind. Both feelings cease to exist when you shut them down.

The men who break out are those who refuse to succumb to pain or shame. They refuse to let shame stop them and instead of conforming to societal norms, they make new records. I do not mean that any one should indulge in vices and feel adequate; I'm referring in the positive light and fight for survival. So what if you had no shoes yesterday and someone saw you walk in those tattered sandals? Instead of being despondent, shake it off. The humiliation only counts when you believe in the superiority of others, seeing them as perfect in your misery. You really have no idea what skeletons they have in their cupboards.

Recently, I was on the phone with a man who's almost fifty years old whom I'll call Steve, and it took quite some time getting through to him. As a matter of fact, I made him my first live student in achieving success in the face of obstacles. He was a broken man. He had lost everything because of one silly mistake. He hit a young man who constantly got on his nerves at work. And of course he went to jail. As at the time he spoke with me, he had been to jail for two weeks and was out; but the case wasn't over. He had court a case coming up and no money. He no longer had a job nor a car. Most importantly, he had no friends. This was an older man with grown kids who should have known better than to hit someone but in a moment of rage he forgot himself and allowed his temper to control him.

The first time I spoke with him, I told him he had to let the shame go. Simple! Wallowing in the dirt doesn't make anyone clean. Until you let the shame go and get some dignity for yourself, you won't make much progress towards your goals. Everyday will be a cycle of regrets and filling your heart with "don't wants." You need to let go of what others think of your cheating spouse or jalopy car and get on with your life. It is more important for you to keep your eyes on your goal than to feel embarrassed before people who do not even like you. I refuse to dissect the reasons why you should actually feel shame. I'll only tell you shame is a distraction and if you want to turn your life around and succeed, you need to sit up quick and do it over. So, whether you're a lady who was jilted at the altar or someone who committed a crime, it's time to put shame away. It's time to dust off the humiliation because it will only sink you. You need to know that winners don't stay shamed.

"And he (Elkanah) had two wives; the name of the one was Hannah, and the name of the other Peninnah: and Peninnah had children, but Hannah had no children. And her adversary (Peninah) also provoked her (Hannah) sore, for to make her fret, because the Lord had shut up her womb. (1 Samuel 1:2&6)

And as he did so year by year, when she went up to the house of the Lord, so she provoked her; therefore she wept, and did not eat. (1Samuel 1:7)

Now Hannah, she spake in her heart; only her lips moved, but her voice was not heard: therefore Eli thought she had been drunken. And Eli said unto her, How long wilt thou be drunken? Put away thy wine from thee. And Hannah answered and said, No, my lord, I am a woman of a sorrowful spirit: I have drunk neither wine nor strong drink, but have poured out my soul before the Lord. Count not thine handmaid for a daughter of Belial: for out of the abundance of my complaint and grief have I spoken hitherto. "Then Eli answered and said, Go in peace: and the God of Israel grant thee thy petition that thou hast asked of him. (1Samuel 1:13-17)

... and the Lord remembered her. Wherefore it came to pass, when the time was come about after Hannah had conceived, that she bare a son, and called his name Samuel, saying, Because I have asked him of the Lord." (1Samuel 1:17-20)

At every point, Hannah could have given up and shut the doors of hope. When the other wife taunted her, she could have walked out on her marriage. When Eli thought she was drunk, that could have been the last straw. Instead she proved that winners don't bow; not to shame and not to pain.

I'm glad she stood, because she taught women like me to keep faith and persevere. She taught me that winners don't quit. And that when the odds are stacked high, you focus on the gain and not the pain because that is the vane that will lead you away from the rain so you can enter your reign.

If you find no reason to lift your head and turn your back on shame, let this be enough for you:

"For your shame, I'll give you double." (Isaiah 61:7)

Ask for help

I had the opportunity to pray with someone over the phone and she was really distraught. She was swimming in bills but it seemed she was mostly worried about her BGE (Baltimore Gas and Electric) bill. She sounded really upset, like she'd been crying and really needed God's help with her finances. I prayed with her but wished I could do more. What I didn't tell her was that I had received a disconnection notice for my own apartment and didn't know how my bill would be paid. I only knew that the money would get in to BGE in time and I would not be left without electricity in the chilly winter when the temperature was often below zero degrees (Celsius). I didn't tell her about my issue but talking and praying with her helped me pick up the pieces of my faith and focus on getting my bill paid. The check got in just in time.

All over the world, people are in need; of money, food, health, companionship, psychological or social support; just name it. In comparison with the world's total population, the proportion of persons who actually have enough to live on and not worry about tomorrow is almost negligible. There is room for more at the top but we all need to pick up the pieces we have left and do something with them.

I deceived myself into thinking asking for help was a sign of weakness but it is not. Refusing to seek help when in need may actually be the weakness. It denotes a form of insecurity and holds little advantage. The worst outcome of seeking help is that you'll get turned down. And if you do, you will have lost nothing but learnt something.

When Bee and other classmates opted to go public with my need, I said no. I meant it. I didn't want them to do it but in the end they did any way. We were four persons, standing to make a decision. I was outvoted 3:1. They saved my dream. When I thanked my colleagues at the end of that day, the money wasn't on my mind; I thanked them for keeping my vision alive. Imagine all I'd have lost if I carried on and refused their help. I almost shudder to think it.

In the midst of difficulty, you need to understand that needing help and asking for it is human. It takes courage to say, *"Man I need help with this."* It is cowardly to accept failure and resort to vices. There is help all around you if you will only see it and reach for it. There is no dignity in stealing or bowing out. You do yourself and offspring an injustice if you accept failure and submit to mediocrity. There is always light at the end of the tunnel; you just have to see it or ask for directions. The silver lining is always in there in the clouds but you may need someone to point out which cloud.

Asking for help does not entail writing appeal letters to everyone you know or asking for funds for daily sustenance. You're much better than that; made of better stuff.

I have been in positions where asking for help was the only thing I could do. It was either I let go of my pride or choked on it. I do not like being turned down and so before I approached anyone for help with any situation, be it explaining an academic concept or even for directions to a certain location, I must have exhausted all other options. With time, I got to understand that this was both foolhardy and a waste of resources. Asking for help is not necessarily asking for funds. A hand up is always better than a hand out.

However, you must know where and when to ask for help. Like we say at Church, not every open door is the right door.

Some would-be helpers may help kill your dream; others will break your spirit; most others will ignore you. In the path of accomplishing your vision, you'll meet many different personalities. By far the most common are the *"It can't be done, give it up"* persons. They are everywhere. Ask such people for directions, and you'll need an extraordinary amount of self-motivation to get out of the pit they'll drop you into. After then, your heart will be filled with doubt and nothing dries up passion faster than lack of trust. The minute you begin to doubt what you saw, that's the beginning of the end.

When I started asking for help, I learnt vital lessons. First, it reinforced my stand that shame was inconsequential and secondly, when people turned me down, which was a real phobia, I found I got stronger and fought even harder.

I was able to turn some of the negativity around me into something positive. The lessons in humility, however, stayed with me. I have a constant Source to Whom I make all supplications. He helps me with everything I succeed at and He strengthens me for more. He is the only Helper to Whom I constantly go, because I trust His judgment. Every counsel given by man has to be approved by Him because I refuse to set myself up for failure. It is normal to need help, guidance and support. Seek it, but only from the right source.

Illustration Format: Shunning Shame and Seeking Help

iFormat 6 (refer to sample iFormat below for exemplary answers)

1. Consider your current goals, situation and vision. Chosen goals may be those already listed in iFormat 1. To make this exercise neater, pick one or two goals from your notes in previous iFormats.

2. What are the painful circumstances surrounding or obstructing your current desires?

3. What needs, incidents, or circumstance makes you feel shame?

4. How can you overcome the shame and stay focused?

5. Have you considered asking for help? Can you reach out to anyone who could help ease some burden so you can focus on achieving your goal?

6. Write out the exact form of help you need and the name of a few persons you can reach out to for help

7. Give them a call immediately. Do not procrastinate

Sample iFormat

1. I want to become a Nurse

2. I was in a relationship but was jilted and I am heart broken. My partner was also my source of support (financial or morale) but I am now all alone

3. I had a baby out of wedlock with my ex-partner and now he is barely responsible. I am ashamed I got involved with someone so hurtful and my friends laugh at me behind my back

4. I will focus on the big picture. I really want to be a nurse because I love to care for helpless people. If I can achieve this, I can make enough money to care for myself and kid. I can also become more respectable, responsible and independent. I feel a surge of hope when I think about this and I need to focus on it more often so I can walk and work towards it.

5. No, I have never considered asking for help but I realize I need help so I am willing to ask.

6. I need a place to stay so I can save on rent money. I also need someone who can watch my child for sometime while I go to school. This will also help me save money by cutting the number of hours in daycare. My grandma lives with my mom now and I think they may be willing to help.

7. I'm calling my mom and grandma this minute. I'll move in as soon as they say yes, so I can get the help I need and go back to focusing on my vision.

CHAPTER SEVEN
GET UP, GO OUT, DO SOMETHING

"A rock pile ceases to be a rock pile the moment a man contemplates it, bearing within him the image of a Cathedral."
- Antone de Saint-Exupery

When Steve called the first time, I was patient with him. I listened to him and heard him pour out his heart. I had never spent the amount of time I did talking with him on the phone with anyone else. I wanted to hear him out. He was a man who had something to say, a burden to offload. It was all well and good during the first call but by the second time he called, reeling out his woes over again, I decidedly acted with a little impatience. This was a man who regretted his actions, was scared of jail and still wanted the finest things of life but was wasting away, whining and pining for what he possessed the power to change or achieve. He reminded me a lot about myself. There was a time when I wanted so much stuff and couldn't help but whine when things didn't go my way. However I learnt that whining is a lazy man's "feel-good" pill. It achieves nothing; solves nothing.

There are people who have been whining for decades. If only their parents didn't die when they did. If only they had been born into wealthy families. If only; if only; if only! I once heard a 42 year-old man say he blamed his father for how he turned out it in life. He was 42 and broke with neither wife nor kids. I would have been a little sympathetic if he didn't drag his long gone parent into his shortcomings. He blamed his father for not bequeathing a financial largesse to him. It was a shameful excuse but he presented it nonetheless. What was worse? He totally believed he made sense! This is how many of us have chosen to live. We have elected to dwell on our insufficiencies regardless of how ridiculous they may be. As a result, we become blinded to our potential.

Through all the pain and drama, I could have chosen to stay home. When I broke my leg, I could have opted for a doctor's report that permitted me to get a leave of absence from school. This way, I would have remained in good legal non-immigrant status while I recuperated at home. It was a simple choice that many would have embraced. If I did that, I wouldn't have reached my goals. Remember, every vision has a timeline. My timing was important. If I did that, chances are that, you wouldn't be reading this book today, drawing inspiration from my success in the face of challenge. Nothing is coincidental in this universe. Even accidents are not coincidental. They are the result of poorly reasoned choices or calculations.

The reason you're still downcast is not because you were born poor. It's not because you graduated with a third class. Bill Gates was a Harvard drop out but he became a billionaire. You need to cease to despair and make a move.

Don't get me wrong. It's okay to feel upset. It's very okay to cry. It confirms your humanity. But it's not okay to continuously dwell in that state of mind; it's impoverishing and unhealthy. On the inside of you lives a champion, let him out.

Until you make a determined choice to succeed, nothing is going to happen; until you make a move, the universe is going to keep waiting.

Get Up

"When you're first thinking through an idea, it's important not to get bogged down in complexity. Thinking simply and clearly is hard to do." -- Richard Branson

Before I got off the phone with Steve during the first call, I asked him to do something. I told him to pick up a piece of paper and put down three things he wanted. He repeatedly said the things he didn't want but never mentioned the things he wanted. This was very significant.

"As a man thinketh in his heart, so is he." (Proverbs 23:7)

For as long as he focused on the things he didn't want, that was all he was going to get. He needed to re-orient his mind into an active state. His current state was docile, passive, inactive! He needed to think and come up with what he truly desired. He understood me, or so I thought; but he didn't do anything about it. He did not write anything down. As far as the universe was concerned, he didn't need anything and so he got nothing; not even a moment's peace of mind.

Within days, he called back again with same complaints. His words were filled with *"Nothing's working for me; I lost my job, I lost everything."* Same old, same old! And so I asked him, *"Did you put pen to paper after the last time we spoke?"* His answer didn't surprise me. I had known instinctively that he hadn't. We ended the second meeting with his promise to write down his desires. He eventually did.

The next time we talked, he said, *"I wrote down a list of the things I wanted, now I feel so much better."* Bam! His focus had moved, from the negative to the positive. He was no longer thinking of what he didn't want, instead his eyes were fixed on what he wanted and that gave him hope. And so I gave him the next task, which was slightly more difficult than the first. I asked him to think carefully about every desire, figure out a way of achieving each one and then write his ideas underneath the appropriate title on the list. For instance, his first goal was to stay out of jail; I wanted him to figure out how to avoid going to jail and then put his thoughts down. He didn't know it then, but that was a powerful task to accomplish. It was the first best step to creating the mental picture that would guide his mind and being to achieve what he wanted.

He needed to think and find a legal way to avoid going to jail for the crime he committed. There were several ways to do so. First, he needed to get a good lawyer. This was probably his first time committing a crime so he would have a previous history of good conduct, and may be able to get his boss, colleagues, and associates to testify on his behalf. This doesn't mean he will go scot-free but if he worked at it, expressing due remorse, he may be able to convince a judge to send him to anger management and community service instead of jail. There were good possibilities but he needed to get up, and think.

Once, he saw himself with a future outside of jail, being free would become a process that will manifest itself through his actions.

The same logic applies to everything a man wants in life. *"I don't want to take buses or cabs anymore"* isn't good enough; you need to want a car. There's a difference. You need to stop focusing on not wanting to be a poor single mom; you have to focus on being a successful woman. Kids don't hinder anyone. Any child can be an inspiration. But you need to focus on the positives and not the negatives; then pick up a pen and write your thoughts down. You have to "get up" out of bed and tell your body to stop feeling weak or succumbing to disease; ask it to be strong. You have authority over every situation, your body inclusive. You have learnt the power in the word of faith and desires of the heart. You know now the power of prayer and the resolution to succeed. Take the first step; get up, write it down.

"Write the vision, make it plain; that they may run that read it; and not wait (you inclusive).

Though the vision is for a while, it will come and not fail." (Habakkuk 2:2)

A vision is only a dream if unaccomplished. Draw up your vision; write it down. Devise the means of accomplishment; write it down. If you do not make your goals plain, you will run around in circles with no direction. Any way will seem like a good door to follow through and you will waste your lifetime chasing shadows. You'll lose vital information necessary for self-motivation and refinement of your vision. If writing down stuff weren't important, we wouldn't have the Bible because then, God would only need to put His laws in our hearts. But to demonstrate the importance of records, the Bible not only tells us of things past, it provides us with insight into the future. This is what guides our paths. This is why every organization worth its weight in salt has a written constitution, by-laws and projections. It is why every visionary company begins the fiscal year with a forecast.

Companies may not be sure of their exact needs but because it is so important to have guidance and direction, they make projections into the future (vision) and these provide guidance for accomplishing goals. Along the way, the vision is modified and refined, but the essence remains the same.

They find out what to take out or retain and even make additions but the path to success is easier because of the set frameworks. I cannot over-emphasize the usefulness of writing down your vision and "how" you intend to accomplish it.

Deciphering the pathway to accomplishment may seem bogus but that doesn't have to wholly be your idea. I have had many abstract ideas lately; ideas that had nothing to do with my area of education or profession; but thank God for the Internet. I say the same to you too, thank God for the Internet! It's as easy as typing in the keywords "how to become successful through" --- (fill in your vision) and hit enter. Solutions will pop up and you can sieve through the answers for different pathways to fulfilling your dream. You can also meditate, talk to people, visit the library, or research through other means.

You don't have to share your original idea with anyone (I advice you not to; not just yet) but get to work. A pen, paper, some motivation, and you're done. You don't have to fill a notebook right away. Heck! You don't even have to fill more than a page right now. It is a workbook or vision book; meaning we will keep adding or removing stuff as time passes. But today, I want you to focus on accomplishing your goals and becoming a success story.

You don't need to think of fresh ideas (if you don't want to). You may already be working on one or several projects and probably getting frustrated. You may be at the verge of giving up something you hitherto thought would be successful. Stop and Think! What do you want from that project? What do you want to see? What's not working right now? What do you want to see it do?

Remember, "what's not working" cannot be entered in our vision book. That's a negative. But knowing what isn't working enables you to see what needs to happen. Now, move your focus from what isn't happening to what should happen and write that down.

When it seemed like graduating from the MPH program was impossible, I wrote down what I wanted to see happen. I wanted to graduate on May 20th 2014, so I wrote it down. I didn't have many options so I went straight to the point. I wasn't passive. I didn't write, *"I want to graduate on May 20th 2014;"* I wrote *"I am going to graduate on May 20th 2014."* If you think these two sentences are the same, you're wrong. Think of two women who walk up to you and one says, *"I* want to have a baby;" the other says *"I am going to have a baby."* Who do you think is closer to having a baby? You're right! Woman number two! She is already carrying her baby! I enjoin you to see yourself as carrying your success. Whether you believe it or not, it's inside of you. You just have to know it, believe it and get moving. First things first!

Get up; make it plain. Write the vision.

"A goal properly set is halfway reached."-Zik Ziglar

Go Out, Do Something

Now, you've written down your goals, your vision, and desires. What next? When Steve was done with his list, his main focus was getting a job but he believed his jail history was a problem. So, I asked him, *"What is the one thing you have desired to do in your life, as your career?"* He told me he had always wanted to go into real estate. He wasn't prepared for my response. I told him, *"Now's the time."* Even over the phone, I could tell he was taken aback. *"Now's the time? How?"* I stopped him before he could recount his challenges and reminded him that he was all he needed to succeed. He wanted to go into real estate business but he didn't have a plan, so we went right back to the basics.

On a fresh page, he wrote *"real estate;"* underneath it, he wrote, *"start my business;"* and then finally he entered, *"register my business name."* This was where he stopped; he told me he didn't have $200 to register his business. I gave him two options. One, *"Walk down the street, talk to your neighbors and acquaintances about mowing their lawns, cutting their children's hair, taking out their thrash or whatever odd job they need and in return, accept a token; save your tokens until you make $200. Two, walk up to Wal-Mart or any other retail store and get a small-time temporary job and put $200 aside from your salary."*

Once he raised the money, I asked him to get business cards (DIY) and offer rental agent services to potential customers while continuing to fill his vision book with improvements. He was to keep developing his business plan and fix his eyes ALWAYS on the big picture.

There is no doubt that after handing out a thousand DIY business cards (refer to iFormat 7) that Steve will receive some links and contacts to begin his business. His vision is to buy and sell houses but today he's to start small by offering rental agent services. We both know he'll finish big but first he has to go out and do something!

Now let's begin with the first goal on your list. Possibly, you want to be very successful. You may have gone through the "get up" stage but are still not sure how exactly to go about reaching for success. At least you know you want to be successful; that's a good start.

"What do you have in your hands?"
"What do you have in the house?"

With the jawbone of an ass, Samson killed a thousand men (Judges 15:15&16). With a jar of oil, the widow who met the prophet Elisha because she was being harassed by her late husband's creditor, was able to pay off her debts and save her sons from going into slavery (2Kings 4:1-7). When the axe borrowed by the prophet's son fell into the water, with a piece of wood, the prophet Elisha made the steel axe float (2Kings 6:5-7). For a time, Goliath harassed the Israelite army but with a stone and sling in the hands of David, he was brought down and David was on his way to being King (1Samuel 17:49-50). When God wanted the children of Israel out of Egypt, He asked Moses, *"What do you have in your hands?"* (Exodus 4:2&3)

The story of how Moses' rod turned into a snake and swallowed up all the rods that were cast by the Egyptian Magicians isn't news. That same rod got the children of Israel across the Red sea, leaving poverty and slavery behind and journeying to become landowners. In every instance, there had to be something for God to bless and multiply. Remember the story of how Jesus fed the 5,000 men? He didn't magically produce the food. He asked his disciple for something to bless. When they gave Him five loaves of bread and two fishes, He gave thanks and blessed it. After feeding 5,000 men, exclusive of women and children, there were 12baskets left (Matthew 14:16-21).

If God in human form did not magically produce the food then, why should it be different now? That is not to say, one cannot have an instant breakthrough or receive amazing gifts on occasion. But if you want something lasting and tangible, there has to be something in your hands/house. The 5,000 men who received the miracle did not keep going back to ask for instant food at every mealtime. Give God something to bless.

This is the same principle that made me ask Steve to "go out." He needed to have something in his hands, something to be blessed. I have been there too many times. So many times I needed money really badly. I was up to my nose in bills with no means in sight of paying them off. On top of that, there had to be food on the table but I could hardly do it. So I prayed fervently and repeatedly for help. I constantly asked God for a breakthrough.

One day, I heard Him ask, *"What do you have in your hands?"* I couldn't think of anything I had in my hands for God to bless. I had nothing to ask Him to multiply. I had a couple of degrees from medical school but I couldn't ask Him to bless those because I was in a foreign country and did not yet have the certification to work in the profession. My hands were empty.

Months later, I was done with studies and awaited my work permit to get a job. For three months, while my application was pending, I wasn't legally allowed to work. I did not even try to get a job. I wasn't ready to break any rules or get in trouble. So I prayed and prayed. I said to God repeatedly, *"God bless me."* It was my request on my knees and while I was about doing chores. Every moment, my needs swallowed up my heart.

Eventually, whenever I got deeply troubled and prayed to God in my heart, I'd hear a gentle voice say, *"Write." "Write? That's it?"* I still had my blog but I was letting myself get choked up with other issues and wasn't paying much attention to it. I have always written stuff from my teenage years but as I earlier stated, publishing wasn't really part of my dream. I have gotten involved in writing stuff for several people and even started a couple of novels but always stopped halfway through. And now, with my B.Sc, MBBS and MPH, He says to me, *"write?"* Wow! I didn't bother to ask Him, *"What about?"* I shut it down and went my way.

It didn't matter that I could have made a ton of money by gearing my talent properly. I was focused on the other things that weren't working. And many people do that. We focus so much on our engineering degrees, we forget we are a natural hand at gardening; we care so much about being an accountant, we forget we are extremely great at and enjoy telling children's stories.

I'm not discouraging anyone from chasing their vision along the paths of their qualifications. As a matter of fact, it is very serving to chase visions that align with our qualifications and passion. But this isn't always the case. When it isn't, don't let anything deter you. Don't sit home for years sending tons and tons of application letters when you can sit down and put other creative skills to work and become the next sensation.

The need to defy limitations got Steve Jobs, Mark Zuckerberg, Bill Gates and many other great entrepreneurs quitting school and focusing on their vision. Ben Carson didn't because his dream aligned with his education. Your mind is your power. Some children have parents who recognize their talents early in life and are then geared to tread the corresponding educational paths. Not everyone gets this opportunity. If you're thinking, *"Well I'm forty-five and my parents never guided me,"* or *"they led me to study courses that fulfilled their own desires,"* you're the one limiting yourself now. We all have different ceilings to break through to reach success. It's only in your mind that your obstacles are greater than those of others. As Zik Ziglar rightly stated, *"Your attitude, not your aptitude, will determine your altitude."* You need to set yourself free and fly.

If I had started writing when He told me to, I'd have become a millionaire before authoring this book. I say that confidently because as soon as I sat down with my computer to begin typing, I know the floodgates that opened. I wish I had listened and gotten myself to "go out and do something" earlier. The bills would have been paid and there would have been excess left.

Before I began writing, my daughter always harassed me about writing her own book. She wanted me to sit with her and work at it. I promised to but I was always busy with something else. One day, while working at a homework in which she was required to make up a story, she "wowed" me and I took notice of her story telling abilities. I saw a book in a story of eight lines and I purposed to give her the time she needed to work at her book. She is likely going to beat me to be first to publish. She has begun a series of children's book for first graders and is about to expand her stories for third-fifth graders. We see a motion picture in her story and have received an investing offer, which we are yet to accept because I want it to be right. Of course, I have positioned myself to be her manager! I am her first employee and content to work as a staff for my daughter because I see the potential.

A few weeks after we started working on her stories, I looked at her and told her, *"You're going to be a millionaire before you're eight."* I meant it; she believed me.

As I work with her, I am involved in a couple of other promising ventures. One already has an investor involved and I have had to put some good ideas on a cool burner so I can concentrate and complete the works I have begun.

The past month, I have been up to my chin in work but I don't mind. I saw a dream, spoke it and believed it; I have written it down and created a mental picture. The picture keeps getting modified, but that's how it goes. Nothing is ever set in stone, except my success (feel free to insert your name here). Now, I am going out, I am doing something; doing whatever it legally and morally takes to ensure that the picture on my mind comes to life. At this point, I can imagine my daughter's face when her story gets a motion picture. Her mental pictures, which I have helped her record, would come alive even better. Those who can't read will see it too! That is how every vision should be. Not made into a film or movie, but inspiring enough to be. You shouldn't rest until you hold your vision in your hands, until you see it, not in your mind but with your physical eyes.

Very few would have believed Steve Jobs and his dream for the entire world to gain access to the Internet. He is not alive today, but his vision is. That is one of the elements of a successful vision. It must outlive you. If you have outlived your vision, get a new one. You must "get up, go out and do something!"

The Potential in Little

So, I ask, if there was so much potential in writing, why didn't I start earlier? The answer is simple, I didn't see it; I placed no value on it. And because of that I stunted my child too. If a farmer considers a yam seedling to be bad and incapable of bearing fruit, he will not bother to plant it. A seed not planted yields no fruit. When the prophet Elisha asked the widow what she had in the house, she could have said *"nothing."* It was just a jar of oil! Probably not even filled to the brim with oil; and meant for cooking. How did a jar of oil translate into an asset that someone could publicly declare? I'm guessing many of us would have answered that question with a, *"nothing, it's just my sons and I."* And if she had said that, I'm thinking her sons would have gone into slavery for sure.

Instead she saw potential in the oil, placed value on it and declared it as an asset. That small jar of oil eventually paid all her bills! The poor widowed woman became a success! I assume she even started an oil business. Yet, many of us are venting and ranting, blaming God, our parents, traitorous friends or relatives, and even witches and all forms of occult powers for our failures. When all along, we have had "a jar of oil" in the house!

Some of us, and I am a prime example of this category, not only have a jar of oil, we also have a "rod" in our hands. You need to set your eyes down and see the potential in the little you have. A jar of oil isn't always physical. It could be your mind. Till it, fertilize it (with God's word), meditate, think; do whatever it takes but bring that mind back to life. A "rod" isn't always literal; it could be your gifts. You may be deft at making hair braids, clothes or whatever else that may require very little to start. Begin to see that gift as capable of buying you a Ferrari (this should be good motivation) and get to work. Let me break it down. Home-based businesses are the roots of some of the most successful businesses in the world. Facebook, cosmetics, and technology companies are fine examples of businesses that were started from scratch, at home.

When Mark Zuckerberg started, he had his computer and his room on campus. Quit marching left, right and center, blaming your poverty on lack of employment. It is not. Your mind is. Employ yourself! My seven year-old just employed me. She got herself a manager who studied at Hopkins! And the Hopkins grad can't boast of her own staff just yet! Rather, she's working for a seven year old! My own daughter becomes my first employer in the United States! Before the end of the week, she's going to sign a contract of employment offering me a salary of $1 per month. Is it too small? Steve Jobs signed on to Apple Inc. for $1 per year. As it is, my little princess will be giving me a much better contract than Steve got! I even got paid upfront!

Oh, you say *"But I don't want to be poor!"* Fail! Now say, *"I am going to be rich."* Then sit down, put down your plans; when you're done, get up, go out and walk towards it. Some of us can gossip for hours and have nothing to show for it. A few women started gossip blogs and earn millions from their blogs monthly. I'm not asking you to go start your own gossip blog. Even if I were, I doubt anyone would be a success at it without the right motivation. Blogging is hard work. Content writing is even harder. Find your niche and I beg you to make it something you love. That's the best way to make it last, and still be content. Learn from Fubu founder, Daymond John, who rightly states, *"don't chase the money."*

When I say, *"go out,"* I do not mean, put on clothes and go outside the house. Going out entails figuring out what to do first, and how to do it. Bloggers and content writers go out everyday without even stepping out of their beds. Some have their workstations (computers) by their bedsides. It's the first thing they see in the morning and the last before going to bed. I've been working intensely for the past month without needing to leave my house. All I've needed is a computer and access to the Internet. Someone offered me office room recently and I turned it down. It seemed like a good idea. In fact, it was a brilliant idea but it was also useless, for now.

I have an office in my home, in my room, or the living room floor. I work better from my "own" office. I am productive here and until I need to, I'm not changing it. It's a waste of resources and I am not indulging in waste.

"To get GoPro started, I moved back in with my parents and went to work seven days a week, 20 hours a day. I wrote off my personal life to make headway on it." Nick Woodman

I see the potential in the space I am in right now; I refuse to give it up. I can work obscene hours from here; I am employed 24hours here. I don't have to bother about day care while I'm in here. I work and work and that's all I need, for now. Some day soon, my office complex will beat every other Governmental organizational complex in my field (Public Health). The dreams are in place; the vision is running but today I am content to start little and walk to the top.

Success may come quickly to those who break the rules but it stays with those who follow the steps. I am no rule breaker. I don't want quick success only; I want lasting success. Perhaps, one of the most meaningful advices I have learnt from is what Mark Cuban was told by his father, *"there are no shortcuts."* So, I build, one step after the other, careful to see the potential in every little seed, to plant it and watch it grow. I don't need $100 to publish my first book; with $20 or even less, I can become an author. The excuse of lack of funds doesn't hold water anymore.

The first time I saw Dr. Myles Munroe's nugget, *"you are your best raw material,"* it stopped me in my tracks but I didn't grasp it. I had a couple of ideas in the works but I needed money to bring any of them to light. How could he say I didn't need resources, friends or connections? How could he say I could become a success from nothing? One of my biggest regrets today, is not meeting this embodiment of wisdom and success before he passed on. Now, I truly recognize and understand the implication of his words, *"you're your best raw material."*

All you need is a "jar of oil" or a "rod" in your hands. Guess what, you have something bigger and better, your mind. See the potential in it; use it. Remember, David didn't need a sword or armor to kill Goliath, the sling and stones in his hand were enough! (1Samuel 17:50).

"Despise not the days of little beginnings." (Zechariah 4:10a)

Illustration Format: Working out your vision

iFormat 7

Case One

Case one is a 23year old female whom I will call Phoebe. Phoebe has never been to College but she completed high school or at least has some elementary education. Phoebe has received some training in salon services (hair fixing) and can also attach artificial nails. She is skilled and talented at what she does. However for the past five years, Phoebe has been looking for a sponsor to help her set up shop. She believes that a store in a highbrow area equipped with at least some of the basic salon commodities/equipment would fetch her enough money to care for her family. She has written several letters to some wealthy members of her local church and even resorted to a soft loan, none of which has borne any fruits. Phoebe is currently despondent and about to loose all hope. She feels her dream is fading away and has no hope of ever raising the money she needs.

Application

Wow! *"Any Phoebes in the house?"* Please take a seat. Your dreams are dependent on no one and the truth is no one owes you anything! It doesn't matter how many appeal letters you write, in the real world, no one wants to befriend a "never do well" yet success has many friends. The aim is to keep your eyes on your vision and challenge the odds in your way by determining to succeed no matter what.

Here's how you can get started (refer to sample iFormat below for exemplary solutions).

1. Take a pen and paper and make a list of all the services you can render. You may have received formal training or they may be inherent gifts that you have developed and for which you could be paid money. List them out. Your list should look something like the one on the sample iFormat below.

2. On a fresh line/page itemize the services that require zero budget to set up or provide. There's plenty on that list. You can refer to the sample iFormat for ideas.

3. Get one plain white poster board sheet (card board). Each sheet costs less than a dollar and can be purchased singly from stationery stores. It measures about 28 by 22 inches and is exactly the type that kids use as poster board for their assignments. Depending on the legibility of your handwriting you may carry out the next step yourself or ask a friend or artist to help you. If you do choose an artist, be sure to explain your financial situation and be persistent until you find someone who can do it for free or close to nothing. This

illustration describes setting up your business from a zero budget so I advocate that you do it yourself, ask a friend or get an acquainted professional to do it for free. This is possible.

4. Cut out the entire poster sheet in small rectangles sized about 3 by 2-inch each. This should yield about a100 small cards. On the alternative, you may purchase a pack of plain DIY business cards from the store. These may be slightly more expensive but are easier to work with.

5. Now write your name boldly across the card on one side. Be sure to include your phone number, email address and contact address.

6. On the other side of the card, legibly print out, "Mobile Salon Service." Underneath this, list out the services itemized in number two of the iFormat. The idea is to begin your business with as little resource as possible and not to limit you to these services. It helps to make the cards a bit decorative and appealing. You could spray a couple glitters on it depending on your choice. When you're done, you'll have 100 customized business cards in your hands. Refer to iFormat figure for sample.

7. Hand out the business cards to friends, colleagues, associates, random individuals you meet at the store, bus

stop, on the bus, anywhere. Whenever you run out of cards, repeat steps 3-7.

8. Keep modifying and strengthening your ideas and abilities. Go on the Internet; learn new ways to provide the services you are good at. Read about your business; develop new ideas; do not be afraid to innovate. Think of ways you can satisfy a client without spending money. Write all your ideas down. Always look at number one on your iFormat. Keep your eyes on the big picture.

9. While you wait for the calls to come in, get a notebook and begin to develop your business plan. Do not think you'll end up as a mobile service provider if your vision is to own a store. However, there is nothing wrong with starting a chain of mobile salon services about town. It's all in your idea and your mind.

10. Watch the calls come in. Go out, do braids and what other services you can provide without a down investment on your part. Keep your prices as low as possible but provide quality service. Listen to your customers carefully and make notes based on their suggestions. Compare products that are available in the market with the needs of your clients. Does the shampoo need less fragrance? Do the oils require more emollients? Continue to research more ideas and develop your business plan.

11. Pray like that's all you can do.

12. Save a good portion (aim at 40%) of payment received for every service rendered. Be sure to pay your tithes. From your income, invest in buying portable salon equipment and merchandise that will enable you to provide all or most of the services listed in number one. Before you set up an onsite store, you may consider getting an extra pair of hands to help you with incoming business.

You're well on your way to establishing an onsite business. Look at your notes comparing available products with customer needs. Begin to think of innovations to fill any lapses. Think of how you can get a customer to choose you over a competitor.

*"If you don't have a reason for people to walk past your competitors and come to your business, then you don't exist."-*Ron Shaich

Good business is always very competitive but don't ever give up. You have now become an entrepreneur and inventor. Congratulations. The sky is your stepping-stone.

This iFormat is applicable to any business for which services do not require an onsite premise. It is useful for starting businesses such as Laundromats, Real Estate, Cleaning, Day Care, Tutoring, Computer graphics, Technological solutions, Cosmetics, Food/pastries; practically any business you can think of. Just fill in the right parameters in each step and follow the directions exemplified. Be innovative and improvise more ideas and guidelines to follow.

Sample iFormat For Success: Mobile Salon Service (Sample answers to the questions above)

1. Services

Long Braids

Short Braids

Natural braids

Hair washing and drying

Hair styling

Hair perms

Hair dyes and processing

Hair cuticle restoration

Scalp treatment

Weaves and attachment of extension

Removal of braids

Attachment of artificial nails (various types)

Attachment of artificial lashes

Hair do for bridal party

Manicures

Pedicures

The list goes on…

2. Pioneer services

Long braids

Short braids

Natural braids

Children's braids

Attachment of artificial lashes (client buys own accessory)

Removal of braids

You can add more to this list.

3. Sample Do It Yourself Business Cards

4. Develop Business Plan

5. Invent own products to better cater to customer needs. For instance, add more Shea butter to improve moisture and resilience in hair care lotions. Mix own shampoo, using simple recipes, but with less fragrance/perfume added.

Case Two

Jeremy Edwards is an innovator. From his childhood, he has toyed with the ide of creating his own inventions. He has received some formal education and over the years has been able to design a new mobile application (or device), or conferred improved functions to an existing device using cheaper methods. For some months, Jeremy has contemplated sourcing for investors to buy into his plan, as he is confident that it will be the next big thing. He is however worried that someone may feign interest but hijack his ideas. This has stunted his progress but he has decided to save up money to pay a patent lawyer to file his application. Presently, it costs between $3,000-$30,000 to pay a good patent lawyer. He has saved up $1,200 but his income is not steady and so he finds it difficult to continue. Even though Jeremy believes his idea revolutionary, he is about to give up and invest his time on something more profitable.

Solution

Hold up "Jeremies!" Before you proceed or give up on your idea, here's what you need to know. It is common knowledge that thousands of patent applications filed and granted by the USPTO never make it to the light of day. That is not to say that your idea is not brilliant but you need to know that the difference between your invention and the ones that do not succeed lies with you. How determined are you? I can only tell you, determination and persistence always pay off?

In order to proceed with this remarkable idea while saving your novelty, I agree that getting a patent is a wise idea. The good news is, you can totally draw up and file a patent application all by yourself. I did.

In order to start, please follow the under-listed directions. Remember, this is only a guideline and requires your full attention and interest.

Illustration Format: Developing and Filing a Patent Application

Get a notebook, and describe your idea in its entirety. Be sure to use the Internet to refine and modify gray areas. Never mind if someone already has a patent for your invention, think of ways to make it better. Be sure to put all of your thoughts down on paper.

Use Google Patents' search engine and look up similar inventions. Be sure to exhaust all published inventions that are similar to yours. Note the differences. Establish the strengths of your inventions.

Using the USPTO or your own country's patent application service, determine the requirements for preparing a patent application. The USPTO office provides clear specifications on the preparation of a patent application. Itemize every specification for each step of the application. The USPTO for instance requires patent application to be described using the following specifications:

i. Title: this is the title of your invention. It should be broad and typically contain about seven words.

ii. Abstract: this is a summarized description of your claims/invention in a maximum of 150 words.

iii. Background: summarize existing inventions and outline the associated problems or shortcomings with these inventions.

iv. Brief summary: provide the general idea of your invention and explain how your invention solves existing problems described in the background of invention.

v. Detailed description: give a full description of your invention, using drawings to illustrate structural and functional applications.

vi. Claims: these are typically prepared by a lawyer but can be done without one if you commit to it. Claims refer to the aspect of your invention that is completely novel and for which you're requesting a patent. Usually, up to 20 claims are allowed per application, with up to three of these claims being major claims.

If preparing patent application as pro se (by self), compare every step of your self-written application with previously published patents. This helps to refine and modify your work to acceptable standards and exposes you to the use of appropriate legal lingo to avoid filing of claims that are limited; but please do not copy anyone's work. Your patent will be denied or you'll expose yourself to lawsuits in the future.

Refine your application with the following guidelines:
i. Search the Internet for FREE patent application templates with which you can compare and sequence the specifications in your application. There are several lawyers who have set up websites with information to help individuals who are unable to hire a lawyer. While they will not physically help with any of your work, their templates are useful for checking your work to see that you have covered all required areas. Continuously proofread your application, checking for grammatical errors and use of language (such as is, must, can etc.) that may restrict your control over your innovated idea; for instance there is a huge difference between "is and may."

By preparing your application yourself, you save thousands of dollars while moving forward with your vision.

ii. Using the specified directives, provide illustrations of processes or functions provided by your invention. It is easier to get a professional to execute this. There is no minimum or maximum number of required pictures or diagrams. While it is not compulsory to provide illustrations, it is strongly advised.

iii. Access the online site of the patent application service, for instance, *uspto.gov,* and fill out required forms. You may apply for a customer number or certificate of action if you so desire. These services are completely free and provide additional privacy and extensive user options when accessing the application site. From saved funds ($1,200), pay the patent application filing, search and examination fee as a small or micro-entity applicant, depending on which status best suits your circumstance. The small and micro-entity fees are only 50-25% of the actual filing fees (a 50-75% discount is given) but this is only available to qualified individuals and with certain limitations. Be sure to review qualifications and renewal before filing the application. It is cheaper to file your application online. This presently costs about $400 for a micro-entity applicant. Only three USPTO forms are required to be submitted while filing online. A phone call to the organization will confirm the forms required for the exact patent for which you desire to apply.

iv. While awaiting the issue of your patent, prepare a business plan; it is now safe to get in touch with those investors and prepare to launch your idea. As with every other business, determination and persistence are keys to success. Practice all of the exercises illustrated (iFormat) in this book from the first chapter, and never forget the big picture. The difference between your invention and thousands others, is you.

CHAPTER EIGHT
THE TANGIBILITY OF VISION

"Hope deferred makes the heart sick; but desire fulfilled is a tree of life." (Proverbs 13:12)

On Monday 20th May 2014, I joined up some 200 plus students to receive my MPH diploma from the Johns Hopkins School of Public Health. My mother and two daughters watched from within the hall; my husband continuously called in to share in the moment. Beside my mother, my friend and Pastor, sat, both beaming with pride and gratitude; both had seen me crawl through fire and rain.

There was something different when I climbed on the stage to receive my scroll from the Dean of the School of Public Health. It was as if the entire staff of the school lifted up their heads to look at me. I saw the Dean of the students' affairs give an approving nod and the Chairman of the MPH program smile at me. I have no idea what the Dean told other graduands when they climbed on the stage but he patted me on the back and said, *"good work."* Instinctively, I knew that he remembered me.

Through my struggle to complete the payment of my tuition at the school, I never met the Dean. My friend Bee, and I had asked to meet him on different occasions but we were told he was out of town. When I wrote him directly, he referred me back to the program office. I believe he was abreast of the entire situation and I have no doubt he remembered. I held my scroll tight and walked down the stage. As I climbed down, I heard someone in a penultimate set call out my name. I looked up and had my picture taken. That night, I went to bed hugging the scroll tightly. This was the proof of my hard work, prayers, tears, pains, and long-suffering. As a teenager, I had dreamed of going to Hopkins. I had written it down and when the time came for me to choose a school to study for my major in Medicine, I researched and found out that for over twenty years, the Johns Hopkins University had been the number one school of public health; likewise, the Johns Hopkins Hospital has been the number one worldwide. It was every doctor's dream to go there. Very few got in. Here I was; through the storm, I had survived to fulfill a lifelong dream. I had completed a goal, reached a vision and well on my path to completing the big picture. It didn't come easy and I value it more because of its cost not only in money but faith.

Many persons would say, *"Well, why didn't you cut your coat according to your size?"* To this I say, *"My vision is tangible in my hands; success is visible in me; there is no coat and no size, only dreams, and hard work."*

"Move fast and break things. Unless you are breaking stuff, you are not moving fast enough". -- Mark Zuckerberg

And oh yes, I wore heels!

I never thought myself a risk taker but I'm proud to find I am. Only risk takers taste a certain level of success. A farmer takes risks when he tills the ground in preparation for the planting season. How does he know that a storm will not wash away all of his precious seedlings once he puts them in the ground? He does not. Yet he toils. He takes the risk anyway and instead of eating all of his precious harvest, he places more seedlings in tilled ground. He doesn't stop there; he takes more risks. He hires laborers, promising them a portion of the harvest that he is yet to see; but he believes. He sees the harvest ahead of planting, watering, tending and whatever else he needs to do. He watches his crops and fences off his farm to prevent goats from eating up the young plants. He keeps at it knowing that someday soon, he'll hold the first fruits of the harvest in his hands and he'll reap enough to not only pay the hire but also take to the market to make profit. These are the processes every vision follows.

Every farmer carries a vision, as do all successful men. Some men succeed beyond the rims of their vision. Some do not, but all men must press and keep faith until hope is no longer deferred and the heart joys from the vision that has become tangible.

The tangibility of vision keeps a man going even in times of despair. Vision becomes tangible when it is fulfilled.

I imagine how Steve Jobs felt when he held the iPad or iPhone in his hands for the first time. I imagine how he felt when he saw the financial report that showed Apple had been completely steered off its course to bankruptcy. Can you imagine how Ben Carson felt when he successfully separated conjoined twins for the first time? Champion! I know the feeling. It is akin to none. But like these men, I still hunger for more. I don't stop dreaming. My early picture isn't accomplished yet. As long as I live, I'll keep dreaming and editing it. There's always room for more. A dead man is one who stops dreaming. I intend to keep living.

For every man, women inclusive, who desires to become successful, your success is incomplete until you hold or see your vision in real time. A vision unfulfilled remains a dream. Each passing day draws you closer to fulfilling your vision. Each passing minute is a good sign. Never let misfortune deter you. Do not sink in fear of passing time. Time is your ally, not your enemy. A delayed vision is not a failed vision; it is a miracle-in-waiting.

Don't be Complacent, Keep Going

"I like thinking big. If you're going to be thinking anything, you might as well think big". -Donald Trump

I agree with Mr. Trump. What's the point wasting a dream? You can start little but never enclose your mind. Let your dream shoot beyond the skies.

I read with dismay how Evan Spiegel turned down a $3billion deal to sell Snapchat to Mark Zuckerberg. *"Who turns down a $3billion dealer deal?"* At the end of the year, Spiegel's invention registered a $50million investment and a valuation close to $2billion! My question was answered. Evan Spiegel turns down a $3billion deal! He has his vision in his hands. His eyes are set on higher sights and he keeps aiming. Very recently, Snapchat asked for a whopping $750,000 as advertiser's fee! 23-year old Spiegel may have well achieved the vision he started off with but he is not letting anything stop him from visualizing more. He isn't subscribing to the "I have arrived" phenomenon.

The names Jan Koum and Brian Acton may not ring bells. If so, these two men continue to achieve one of their desires, that despite being tech billionaires, they continue to live a life away from the limelight. Jan and his mentor Brian left Yahoo to build the messaging application, Whatsapp. Early 2014 saw Jan and his partner become billionaires19 times over when Facebook bought the app for $19billion dollars. Although most of the money is in stock, both men are still billionaires in cash. Theirs is an amazing story of how quickly life can turn around through dedication to one's vision. Today, Jan is on the Facebook Board of directors, a long shot from the poor immigrant who survived on food stamps. Today, they hold their vision in their hands, yet they haven't stopped.

There is a dream that stirs within your soul. It is the vision that requires your passion to come alive. Inside of every man lives a champion, waiting for its chance to fight and prevail. At the end of every battle, a conqueror returns home to rest.

He desires refreshment but his heart is fixed on one thing only; that is, to remain a champion.

"He teacheth my hands to war; so that a bow of steel is broken by mine arms." (2 Samuel 22:35)

The Williams's sisters broke into the tennis world and have dominated it for years. They have won every recognizable prize and have repeatedly occupied the number one position, often edging out other sportswomen to occupy both the number one and two positions. They have both tied for the number one position and are considered a phenomenon in the world of tennis. These young women, Serena and Venus, have persevered and fought hard to hold and keep their crowns. The only person who doesn't fear Serena on the court is Venus, and vice-versa. They hold their vision and are yet unstoppable, in a field where it should have been difficult to reign. They have continued to rule the game through persistence. Like other humans, their distractions have been intense but they consistently rise above and prevail against all odds.

To everyone out there, struggling and losing hope because the battle has been intense, I want you to know that hurdles are real to every champion. He may bend over to dodge the sword of a persistent enemy but he lifts his head up and gains control of the war because of who he is. He does not bow to shame or pressure. He sees that he is a victor and presses forward to gain the crown. He fights, until he holds his vision in his hands, and then he can lift up his eyes to heaven, knowing he has become a conqueror, against all of life's odds. He gives a shout of victory and roars like the lion that he is. Legends are not faint hearted. They are risk takers and they are persistent. They don't give up. They know without the slightest doubt that though it tarries, the vision must be borne. They hope and dream, and one day they see and hold the prize. Success comes to those who fight.

"Impossible is nothing!"

SUCCESS COACH

1. Make a list; itemize your desired goals. Keep it simple

2. Prioritize; erase irrelevant desires or goals

3. Define process: how you can achieve number two

4. What do you have in your hands: talent, job, resources, or ideas, to aid in achieving your vision/goals (this may be number one)

5. Research: find out how to maximize your resource or put your talents/passion to best use; use the Internet; think; ask questions.

6. Modify: keep editing; explore existing markets and adapt vision to suit future needs

7. Get going: remain persistent; do not abandon process.

8. Launch your vision

9. Remain inspired in the face of discouragement; pray; nurture your dream

10. It's okay to take a break to re-strategize and build up a better resolution

11. Watch your vision come alive, see it with your eyes and hold it in your hands.

Go, be a champion!

BIBLIOGRAPHY FOR BIOGRAPHIES

1. Adweek. Snapchat Is Asking Brands for $750,000 to Advertise and Won't Budge. http://www.adweek.com/news/technology/snapchat-asks-brands-750000-advertise-and-wont-budge-162359

2. Bio. Ben Carson. Ben Carson Biography. http://www.biography.com/people/ben-carson-475422

3. Bio. Mary Kay Ash Biography. http://www.biography.com/people/mary-kay-ash-197044#synopsis

4. Bio. Mark Zuckerberg Biography. http://www.biography.com/people/mark-zuckerberg-507402.

5. Bio. Steve Jobs Biography. http://www.biography.com/people/steve-jobs-9354805

6. Business Insider. 12 Successful Entrepreneurs Share The Best Advice They Ever Got. http://www.businessinsider.com/entrepreneurs-best-advice-2013-12#

7. Forbes. Facebook Tried To Buy Snapchat For $3B In Cash. Here's Why. http://www.forbes.com/sites/jeffbercovici/2013/11/13/facebook-wouldve-bought-snapchat-for-3-billion-in-cash-heres-why/

8. Forbes. The Rags-To-Riches Tale Of How Jan Koum Built WhatsApp Into Facebook's New $19 Billion Baby. http://www.forbes.com/sites/parmyolson/2014/02/19/exclusive-inside-story-how-jan-koum-built-whatsapp-into-facebooks-new-19-billion-baby/

9. Forbes. The Rockefellers: The Legacy Of History's Richest Man.

http://www.forbes.com/sites/carlodonnell/2014/07/11/the-rockefellers-the-legacy-of-historys-richest-man/

10. Forbes. WhatsApp Founders Become Billionaires In $19 Billion Facebook Deal.

http://www.forbes.com/sites/ryanmac/2014/02/19/whatsapp-founders-become-billionaires-in-19-billion-deal-with-facebook/

11. Giants for God. RG LeTourneau – Earthmoving Innovator.

http://www.giantsforgod.com/rg-letourneau/

12. Success Motivation Institute. Paul J. Meyer.

http://www.success-motivation.com/index.php?option=com_content&view=article&id=25

13. USPTO. Nonprovisional (Utility) Patent Application Filing Guide. A Guide to Filing a Utility Patent Application.

http://www.uspto.gov/patents/resources/types/utility.jsp

14. Wikipedia. The Free Encyclopedia: Asa Candler.

http://en.wikipedia.org/wiki/Asa_Griggs_Candler

15. Wikipedia. The Free Encyclopedia: Ben Carson.

http://en.wikipedia.org/wiki/Ben_Carson

16. Wikipedia. The Free Encyclopedia: Malala Yousafzai.

http://en.wikipedia.org/wiki/Malala_Yousafzai

17. Wikipedia. The Free Encyclopedia: Mark Zuckerberg.

http://en.wikipedia.org/wiki/Mark_Zuckerberg

18. Wikipedia. The Free Encyclopedia: R.G Letourneau.

http://en.wikipedia.org/wiki/R._G._LeTourneau

19. Wikipedia. The Free Encyclopedia: Steve Jobs. http://en.wikipedia.org/wiki/Steve_Jobs.

20. Wikipedia. The Free Encyclopedia: Tyler Perry. http://en.wikipedia.org/wiki/Tyler_Perry

COME TO JESUS

"Come to me and I will give you rest—all of you who work so hard beneath a heavy yoke. Wear my yoke—for it fits perfectly—and let me teach you; for I am gentle and humble, and you shall find rest for your souls; for I give you only light burdens."

Accept the altar call and let Him be your Lord and Savior…

Lord Jesus, I know that I have sinned;
I know that You're God and You died to save me;
I believe that You rose from the dead and are ascended into Heaven. I believe that Your blood can wash away my sins and make me whole; please forgive me of my sins.
Today, I accept You as my Lord and Savior.
Come into my heart and be the Master of my life.
I am redeemed by Your blood.
Thank you Jesus.

In Jesus' name…. AMEN.

AUTHOR BIO

 Elohor Okpeva-Effiong is a Medical Doctor and Public health practitioner, born & raised in Nigeria. She is a firm believer in God and a proclaimer of the gospel of Christ. She undertook her undergraduate education at the University of Port Harcourt, Nigeria from where she obtained the Bachelor of Science (B.Sc.) in Human Anatomy, and the Bachelor of Medicine, Bachelor of Surgery (MBBS) degrees.

She studied and obtained the Master of Public Health (MPH) degree at the Johns Hopkins University, Baltimore MD, USA; and holds several post graduate certificates in Global health, Humanitarian assistance and training certificate in Business management.

She is also a charismatic and motivational speaker. She is a member of Salvation Ministries International where she volunteers as a counselor, prayer line, and health/media personnel. She is happily married with three beautiful kids.

www.iformat4success.com

achievingsuccess@iformat4success.com

author@iformat4success.com

Free personal coaching.

www.ingramcontent.com/pod-product-compliance
Lightning Source LLC
Chambersburg PA
CBHW051902170526
45168CB00001B/206